THE BOOK ON MERGERS AND AQUISITIONS

JAMES SCOTT

Publisher:

New Renaissance Corporation
73 Old Dublin Pike, Suite 10 # 142
Doylestown, PA 18901

www.newrenaissancecorporation.com

DISCLAIMER AND/OR LEGAL NOTICES

The information presented herein represents the views of the author as of the date of publication. Because of the rate with which conditions change, the author reserves the rights to alter and update their opinions based on the new conditions.

The author has strived to be as accurate and complete as possible in the creation of this report, notwithstanding the fact that she does not warrant or represent at any time that the contents within are accurate due to the rapidly changing nature of the Internet.

While all attempts have been made to verify information provided in this publication, the author assumes no responsibility for errors, omissions, or contrary interpretation of the subject matter herein. Any perceived slights of specific persons, peoples, or organizations are unintentional

TABLE OF CONTENTS

How to negotiate the best deal

How to analyze synergy between the target company
and your company

Why being a publicly-traded company makes it easier
to facilitate M and As

Articles of association

Bylaws

Recent shareholder communications

Certificates of operating authorization

Minutes of board and other meetings

Copies of stock certificates

Copies of warrants

Copies of options

Stock register

Shares issued and when

Holdings by percentage

Outstanding preferred stock
Any applicable covenants

Outstanding warrants, options and other securities
Other securities
Options and other employee benefits
Employee stock ownership

Audited financials since inception
Balance Sheets
Cash flows
Accounting methods and practices
Revenue recognition policies
Management Accounts
Budgets and projections
Business plan
Accounts receivable analysis
Accounts payable analysis
Pricing plans and policies
Revenues and margin by product
Extraordinary income/expenses
Analysis of material write downs
Bad debt summary
Any outstanding contingent liabilities
Any external financial reports/studies

Federal tax returns for 3 years
Local or state tax returns for 3 years

ABOUT THE AUTHOR

James Scott is a consultant, author and lecturer on the topics of IPO facilitation, corporate structuring, Private Placement Memorandum authoring and Mergers and Acquisitions strategies. Mr. Scott has authored multiple books such as 'The Book on Mergers and Acquisitions', 'The Book On Mergers and Acquisitions', 'The Book on PPMs: Regulation D 504 Edition', 'The Book on PPMs: Regulation D 505 Edition', 'The Book on PPMs: Regulation D 506 Edition' as well as several templates that make the process of completing complicated S1 and PPM docs as easy as 'point and click' for entrepreneurs and corporate CEOs.

Mr. Scott is a member of several economic think tanks that study diverse aspects of legislation concepts that effect corporations worldwide such as: Aspen Institute, Chatham House: Royal Institute of International Affairs, The American Enterprise Institute, Economic Research Council, American Institute for Economic Research, The Manhattan Institute and The Hudson Institute among others.

To contact James Scott visit the 'Contact Us' page at the New Renaissance Corporation publishing website at: www.newrenaissancecorporation.com

PREFACE

This manual is designed as a resource for people involved in all facets of mergers or acquisitions. The steps involved in such transactions are thoroughly explained. It is our goal that, after having gone through this manual, you'll know how to handle each step in the merger and acquisition process.

Mergers and acquisitions (M&As) have played a major role in the expansion and consolidation of business organizations across the globe. Recently, M&As have become important in influencing market forces. This is one reason for the dramatic increase in the number of mergers over the last decade. M&A transactions are worth a considerable amount in terms of dollars as well as in terms of number of transactions. In 1998, there were more than $1 trillion in mergers and acquisitions in the United States alone, more than 7,500 transactions.

After reading this manual, all stakeholders should have adequate information on how to handle the merger or acquisition transaction. Mergers and acquisitions are not the same thing, and it is important to understand the difference. One difference is speed. If investors need the transaction to be completed in a short amount of time, then an acquisition will likely be the most appropriate. That is assuming that the assets of the acquired company are a strategic fit to the new owner's existing company.

Some business investors think that internal development is a good strategy. One reason why investors prefer mergers or acquisitions to creating a company from scratch is that these are faster ways of entering the market or expanding into new markets. In some cases, a market opportunity may have passed if a company waits to ramp up its own internal operation to meet the demand.

All regulatory requirements of a merger or acquisition are listed in this manual. When a merger involves millions of dollars, companies must adhere to federal antitrust statutes, state laws and Securities and Exchange Commission (SEC) regulations. There are additional requirements for non-public transactions.

1
HOW TO IDENTIFY M & A TARGETS

I. HOW TO FIND M & A TARGETS

You need to know how much a company is worth to be able to judge its value as a merger or acquisition. Therefore, the very first step in a merger and acquisition process is calculating the market value of the target company. You also need to calculate an estimated future value of the company. Looking at these two values is the easiest way to understand if a firm is worth merging with yours or acquiring outright. To do this, you will need to spend a considerable amount of time studying the target company's business history. Check on the products manufactured by the firm, its capital requirement, the value of its brands and its organizational structure. Review every aspect of the target company.

II. HOW TO NEGOTIATE THE BEST DEAL

According to Financial Directions Inc. (2009), an organization must consider a number of factors before entering into a merger or acquisition. They have identified three primary groups of issues:

Pre-Acquisition Issues

Post-Acquisition Issues and

Administrative Issues

In the pre-acquisition phase, you evaluate the organization to be purchased by performing due diligence. This step takes place long before the letter of intent (LOI) or the purchase agreements are signed. At this stage, the purchasing company is required to point out the known and any potential liabilities. It is a good strategy to identify all the issues that need to be sorted out before the purchase takes place.

The methods elaborated in this manual will be useful in guiding the board of directors through negotiating the acquisition transaction. By following these methods closely, you will be in a position to get the best deal for your shareholders. According to Financial Directions Inc. (2009) and Kuenyehia (2010), the following strategies are essential to the proper merger and acquisition negotiation:

Establishment of a Special Negotiation Committee

Establishing a special negotiation committee is the first step for a company looking to complete a merger or acquisition transaction. Such a committee should be made up of members with a lot of experience in M&A matters and, above all, have no vested interest in the company being discussed. It is a good idea to include leading professionals from compensation, benefits and payroll as well as representatives from other disciplines within the company that may be affected by the merger or acquisition. The committee should also include an accountant, an experienced M&A lawyer, an investment banker, a valuation expert and a tax advisor. All parties must be free from conflicts of interest. The goal of the negotiators is to arrive at the most logical price for the acquired company and to get the best terms in the acquisition proposal. Snow (2012) maintains that the merger committee is one of the most important aspects to a M&A. Business owners attempting to complete the merger transactions alone will almost inevitably meet with disaster.

Keep in mind that the negotiation process is simply a means to an end and not the end itself. The committee members will succeed more easily if they outline their most important goals right from the start. The committee's primary goal should be to work towards obtaining the best deal possible for the company's shareholders. Basically, the firm's objectives will be met when the committee understands the core values and sticks to those values throughout the negotiation process. Knowing when to stop and when to hold firm on key issues, like future investments, price and integration, is paramount. *Engage the most Competent Advisors*

Step number two is to engage the most competent advisors possible. At this point in the M&A process, you will be dealing with highly sensitive information. Your company must hire people with the best skills in areas of tax, sales, process design and implementation, law, due diligence, valuation of the company, financial evaluation, compensation and regulatory arrangements. By using competent advisors, you will know as much as you can about the proposed acquisition before you complete the transaction.

Avoiding Conflicts of Interest

It is essential that no member of the committee have any conflict of interest regarding the M&A transaction. All people working on the merger or acquisition must be questioned to that effect. A quick consideration must be made if any conflict of interest is cited. The aim of your company is to eliminate any form of bias (or appearance of bias) that could be caused by conflicts of interest. When in doubt, it's always better to err on the side of caution.

An independent committee makes it possible for your company to base its decision on corporate advantage rather than external influences or considerations from politicians and other people with a vested interested in the transaction.

Determination of price via thorough review

The best prices and best terms are arrived at through carrying out proper reviews. This is the process that determines whether the price offered makes sense from a business standpoint. At this stage, the committee should use the services of investment bankers, advisors and legal experts to set an appropriate price. This includes reviewing a lot of varied information. Just a few such sources include company Websites, trade show material, trade publications and talking to the designated team of advisers.

This stage involved a lot of different activities, including:

Conducting a detailed review of the target company's current and past financial results

Scrutinizing financial forecasts related to company business, assets, cash flow, prospects and liabilities

Discussing future company prospects and goals with top management at the target company

Checking on the company's current price per share and making a comparison with other shares of similar companies traded on the same stock exchange

Reviewing company projections for at least the next two years

Reviewing company business plans

Looking at the market for the company or preferably, the replacement value of company assets

Analyzing whether a better price might be obtained in the future

Determining the impact of suppliers, managers and customers, among other people related to the company

Finding out whether there are any regulatory or legal issues raised by the proposed transaction

The committee should not hesitate to reject the offer if they find out that the price is inadequate or if the time is wrong for getting the best price or the best terms.

Use the Closed Auction Strategy

Using the closed auction strategy is a good choice for any company. Using this method, all interested parties are required to buy shares and make a sealed bid by the predetermined deadline. The committee is responsible for issuing a memorandum describing the offer to the prospective bidders. Long before the bidding process starts, the special committee will need to draw up a contract for all prospective bidders. This will allow the bidders enough time to do their due diligence and be able to submit their bids together with any comments. In a closed auction, there is more than one round and more than one bidder. It may even be more desirable to choose a closed auction in cases where there is

only one bidder. This way, the bidder(s) don't know whether there are any other interested bidders. Therefore, they always put forward their best bid. With a closed auction, the
committee must negotiate with bidders to encourage them
to put forward higher bids. *Keep Proper Records and Apply
the Front Page Test*

This sixth step requires keeping clean records as well as
practicing the 'front page' test. In whatever the committee
does, it must remember that all its actions might eventu-
ally be challenged in court. Therefore, all committee meeting minutes should be kept as core records. These minutes
should clearly state what has been done, who did it, and
how it was done. All oral and written material used during
presentations should be stored with the minutes alongside
any advice and recommendations of the experts.

The appointed advisors should play a key role in preparing
the legal, financial documents and any other presentations
for the committee. This is necessary to help committee members make well-informed decisions. The committee must be
reminded to keep detailed, accurate records of their pro-
ceedings because they can serve as a great memory booster
should the transaction ever be subject to litigation. It will
also be evidence that due care was taken. The materials must
be compiled for every meeting and be available in written
format of all issues that were debated during the meetings.

You must understand that the committee will have many
choices to make as well as being subject to pressures from
litigants, trade unions and even politicians. That is why the
committee is advised to apply the "front page" test. That is,
they should consider how the headline would likely read if
their decisions were reported on the front page of the *Wall
Street Journal,* the *Financial Times* or another reputable news

paper or magazine. This step helps to make sure that the committee's decisions are perceived reasonably by people outside of the company, how decisions could be explained and the effect of such decisions.

Negotiate the terms

The next step is to draft a letter of intent that caps the purchase price and to then begin due diligence. The seller should identify price, terms and conditions. It is worth knowing that the seller's leverage is greatest at the LOI stage. After the letter of intent, the lawyers take over the process.

The Committee must be Vigilant and Focused

The committee needs to learn to stay focused at all times in their dealings. The committee members should remember that there is no transaction until the deal is closed, and in some special cases, even later. New issues will virtually always come up even after the deal is signed. These issues can have a negative impact on some aspects of the deal, even putting the deal in danger of collapsing. Therefore, it is important to be alert and be ready to act quickly to save the deal.

Close the Deal

According to Wilson (2012), the buyer should set tight deadlines so as to force seller errors. It is a good idea to recheck the target and deal criteria after the due diligence stage. Sellers should be prepared for the fact that the deal may not close. Sellers must keep talking to the buyer through multiple lines of communication. In all cases, the buyer must hold to a unified message. Remember that a strong business is brought around by a strong negotiating position.

III. HOW TO ANALYZE SYNERGY BETWEEN THE TARGET COMPANY AND YOUR COMPANY

According to Towers Perrin (2008), it is very important to analyze the synergies between the target company and the purchasing company. Check out whether assumptions regarding cost and revenue synergies are valid, and investigate any liabilities that are expected to arise from such things as golden handcuffs, customer overlap and pension plans, just to name a few examples. Find out if there are any major integration costs such as those associated with IT systems and other shared integration services.

According to Evans (2010), understanding the synergies of a merger or acquisition increases the probability of a successful merger. In a merger, there is an underlying principle that states that 2+2=5. That means that if company A is valued at $2 billion and company B is valued at $2 billion, merging the two companies will lead to a new company valued at $5 billion dollar. That means that merging two companies creates additional value. This added value is called synergy. Evans (2000) further argues that there are three forms of synergies.

Cost of Capital: When two companies combine in a merger or acquisition, they face a lower cost of capital.

Revenues: Merging two companies leads to higher revenues than when the two companies operate separately.

Expenses: Expenses are generally lower when two companies merge than when the two companies operate independently.

The largest source of synergy for two merging companies is the lowered expenses. That is why many mergers are inspired by the possibility of realizing dramatically-reduced operating costs. These reduced expenses are usually a result of eliminating redundant services between the two firms, such as human resources departments and IT support.

Of course, there are other strategic reasons why people engage in mergers. Gap filling is another common reason for entering into a merger agreement. To illustrate the importance of gap filling in a merger, let us offer an example. If one company has some weaknesses, such as poor distribution, it can merger with another company with a strong distribution system. The combined company will be more powerful and will be able to benefit from a strong distribution system sooner than if the original company attempted to ramp up its operation. This merger will help the combines company survive in the market place.

Another key reason for entering into a merger is positioning. Strategic positioning is necessary to be in a better position to take advantage of future opportunities. For example: a broadband service company might merge with a telecommunication company. This arrangement improves the combined company's position for future business.

Broader Market Access

When a company acquires a foreign company, it gets quicker access to new markets.

It may also be cheaper to acquire another company than investing internally. As an illustration: suppose that a company wants to expand into the fabrication business and there is another company with idle facilities. It makes sense and costs less to acquire that company than to build a new facility.

Diversification is yet another reason for merging with another company, especially if a company needs to smooth out its earning. After merging with a company in a different industry, the combined company aims to become more profitable and to ensure consistent growth. This is particularly well-suited for those corporations operating in well-established industries where there is little opportunity for future growth. A merger or acquisition can lead to short-term growth in profitability.

Undervalued Investments

When analyzing the synergies between two companies, focus on target companies that are undervalued. This will usually make a good investment for the purchasing company.

IV. WHY BEING A PUBLICLY-TRADED COMPANY MAKES IT EASIER TO FACILITATE AN M & A

A variety of documents are needed to form a corporation after a merger, such as the articles of incorporation. This document requires the applicant to set the number of shares that the new corporation is allowed to offer. This number must be larger than zero, according to the California Secretary of State. Because of this, it is easier for a publicly traded corporation to facilitate a merger. Evans (2000) maintains that publicly-traded companies are easier to deal with because many private corporations are full of excesses that make it more difficult to arrive at an accurate valuation. Some examples of those excesses by private companies include:

Over-generous bonuses, travel privileges and other perks

Unnecessary motor vehicles and other assets

Consultants for unnecessary services because they have strong ties to company management

Unusually high salaries

Family members listed on the payroll who are not offering any useful service to the company

The sole objective for the purchasing company should be to get an accurate picture of what values and profits will be after the merger.

2
DOCUMENTATION

a. Verifying operating documentation is also important to make sure that new staff can run the business, if necessary.

b. Items to check:

I. ARTICLES OF INCORPORATION

In order to form a professional, stock or closed corporation, a company must file articles of incorporation with the Secretary of State in the company's home state. The company can use form ARTS-GS for a general stock company as a result of a merger. To form a closed corporation, form ARTS-CL is more appropriate. A company can also opt to draft their own articles of incorporation. California's Secretary of State maintains that these forms meet the minimum statutory requirement. However, it is advisable to seek legal advice from a private attorney about the specific needs of a merger or acquisition and/or if there are any additional provisions.

Some states require that to form a stock corporation through a merger, the proposed name must contain the word "corporation" "limited" or "incorporated" or an abbreviation of any of these three words. There are also name-style require-ments associated with forming a professional corporation. Specific requirements vary depending on the laws govern-ing the profession under which the corporation will be work-ing. These requirements are available by contacting the state board or agency that controls your profession or industry.

If you compose your own articles of incorporation, make sure that you include the name of the corporation in the title of the document. The name must be written exactly as it ap-pears in the articles. If you fail to do that, the articles of in-corporation will be returned to you without being filed. The corporate purpose should also be included in the articles of incorporation, unaltered in any manner.

Service of Process

The proposed corporation after a merger is required to name an agent for service of process. The agent can be a person or a corporation. If it is a person, you will also be required to supply the agent's street address. That means that the agent must be a resident of the state in which you file your articles of incorporation. A corporation that is active in the new company's home state and that has filed a certificate is required by section 1505 to also act as your agent for ser-vice of process. The agent will be responsible for accepting service of process in the event the proposed corporation is sued. The proposed corporation must seek consent from the agent prior to listing the name. A corporation can never act as its own agent of service of process. Remember that you can only list one agent.

Under the articles of incorporation, you will also be required to list the corporate addresses. The proposed corporation after a merger is supposed to list the street address of the merger and not its postal address. You will also need to list the number of shares that the corporation is allowed to issue to the public. This number has to be greater than zero. Finally, remember that each incorporator must sign the articles of incorporation. This statement of information needs to be filed within 90 days of filing the articles of incorporation.

Articles of Incorporation for Nonprofit Corporations

Nonprofit corporations (also called not-for-profit corporations) are those organized for educational, religious, recreational, social and charitable reasons. They differ from for-profit companies in that they are forbidden by law to distribute earnings to shareholders. (They cannot make a profit.) There are cases when it is necessary for two such organizations to merge into one formidable corporation in order to improve efficiency and service delivery. One type of nonprofit corporation is religious organizations that are organized to operate a church or carry out other religious duties. These are called nonprofit religious corporations.

A second type of nonprofit organization is organized to carry out charitable duties. Many states allow these corporations tax exempt status. To form such corporations, in most states, you will be required to file the articles of incorporation, following state laws.

Fees for Filing the Articles of Incorporation

The fees for filing the certificate of incorporation vary from state to state. In most states, the fee is nominal. For example, in California, the fee is just $1.

II. ARTICLES OF ASSOCIATION

In some jurisdictions, the articles of association are known as the articles of incorporation. The company constitution is made up of the articles of association and memorandum of association. The contents of this document include the work of directors, the type of business the company will engage in, and even the extent to which the shareholders will have control over the board of directors. All companies should have some regulations and rules in place to govern the company's affairs. The duties and rights of all members forming a company should be outlined. The articles of association are required to be filed at the registrar of companies in the company's home state.

The articles of association should include:

The powers of directors and other officers as well as the voting practices of the shareholders

How the company business will be performed

How changes in internal regulations will be achieved

The powers and duties of the company and the members listed in the articles of association

The articles of association is not only binding for the current members of the company, but also on those who will join the company in future. The articles of association dictate how hiring process is done, how the existing members should be treated and how the legal representatives should handle the affairs of the company. Company members are bound to the company immediately when they sign the document. This is actually a contract between the company and its members. All the rights and duties of the members are listed so that the running of the company becomes easier and more straightforward. The company also has some obligations that it must fulfill towards its members.

The articles of association or incorporation are frequently referred to simply as the articles, and it can be abbreviated and capitalized to represent the full term. For LLC companies, the articles of association are called the articles of organization.

The following are the topics covered in the articles of association. They should be checked thoroughly during the merger and acquisition process.

Appointment of directors: This clearly indicates if there are shareholders who dominate the rest of the contributors.

Transferability of shares: a clear way of assigning rights is outlined here.

Management decisions: An outline of who makes major decisions, such as the directors or the company founder

Directors meeting: The percentage of vote required and the quorum necessary to start the meeting

Issuing of Shares/stock: All the voting rights are explained here.

Special voting rights of the company Chairman and how he/she is elected

Dividend policy: the percentage of profits which is to be declared when the company makes a profit or what is to be done in cases of a loss

What is to happen if the company is to be shut down

The right of refusal: this is the counter bid and purchase rights of the Chairperson.

It is a common practice for companies to be run by the shareholders. This is made more convenient by giving the day-to-day management to the directors who are elected from time to time. The members of the Board of Directors are elected by the shareholders during the annual general meeting (AGM). The number of directors needed depends on several factors, including the statutory requirements and the size of the company. The Chairman is usually a popular outsider or sometimes he or she is one of the executives working for the company. The directors may be employees of the company or those elected from outside of the company. The shareholders are also permitted to nominate independent directors. These are the nominees who are elected during the annual general meeting session. After the elections, the Board of Directors is responsible for running the company. That means that the shareholders' active role in the company will cease until the next annual general meeting. The name of the company, the company street address and the founding directors cannot be changed except by vote of the shareholders at the annual general meeting. The shareholders are also responsible for appointing the company's internal and external auditors during the AGM. The Board of Directors meets several times during each fiscal year. There needs to be a predetermined number of directors present (called a quorum) for the meeting to begin. In the event of a voting tie, the Chairman uses his or her vote to break the tie. All the resolutions by the board are subject to a vote. The chairperson must always be present at the board meetings and, in most meetings, decisions are made by a show of hands. Counting written votes is occasionally used. The shareholders are also involved in voting. The other special voters are the 'proxy' who is authorized by shareholders. The board of directors can make two types of decisions--special resolution and ordinary resolution.

III. BYLAWS

An acquisition or a merger is a combination of two corporations where one of the corporations is fully absorbed by another corporation. The target company loses its corporate identity while the purchasing company retains its identity. Therefore, a merger extinguishes the merged corporation while the surviving corporation assumes all the rights, liabilities and privileges of the merged corporation. Note that there is a difference between a merger and a consolidation. In the latter, two corporations are required to lose their separate identities and form a wholly new corporation.

Federal as well as state laws govern mergers and acquisitions. These regulations are necessary because of concerns that mergers can lead to the elimination of competition between the merging firms. Such concerns are more serious in cases where the two merging firms are strong rivals. The federal and state courts make a presumption that such business arrangements are likely to put restrictions on output and lead to increased prices in the market. Therefore, such mergers are presumed to play a role in reducing competition. That is the main reason why the government carefully scrutinizes any such proposed mergers.

The US government and individual states have relaxed these anti-trust laws in recent years, allowing for more mergers with complete corporations. The main reason for this change is that mergers and acquisitions are believed to lead to plenty of benefits, such as getting better management for the newly-formed corporation as well as more properly-utilizing assets in either of the two participating corporations. There are also economies of scale to be gained in many mergers as well as improved quality and increased productivity. A business climate friendly to mergers also encourages entrepreneurs to form new firms since they know that those firms can be acquired easily through mergers and acquisitions at higher prices. Despite these developments, there is still an antitrust merger law aimed at preventing those transactions which truly hinder competition among the participating firms. Because of this, the government gets involved in all mergers as soon as the merger is first proposed. The courts and other enforcement agencies play a crucial role in forecasting future market trends plus any anticipated effects of a proposed merger or acquisition.

Merger Procedures

The Secretary of State is charged with setting corporate merger procedures in his or her particular state. These procedures are contained within the bylaws of that state. In a general case, the board of directors from each of the merging companies is required to pass a resolution that adopts a plan of merger at the initial stages of the merger process. Such a resolution must clearly state the names of corporations that are party to the merger or acquisition and the proposed names of the newly merged corporation. The method of converting the shares of the two participating corporations must also be clarified at this point. The resolution will state the legal provision to which the corporations agree. Then the bylaws require that each corporation notify all the shareholders about a planned meeting during which the shareholders will be required to approve or disapprove the merger. In case the majority of shareholders approve the plan, the directors will be required to sign the merger papers and file them with the Secretary of State in the company's home state. In return, the Secretary of State will issue a certificate that authorizes the operation of the new corporation.

Though each state's laws are somewhat different, a number of state bylaws allow the involved directors to abandon the plans to merger at any time before signing the final papers. There are also some states with more liberal laws that do not require the surviving company to submit its plans to shareholders for approval when absorbing another company. In such states, the approval is necessary when the certificate of incorporation demands such approval.

If the merger is formed by companies from two different states, the involved corporations must obey all the bylaws in both of their respective states for the merger to be upheld. There are some states which require that the shares of shareholders who vote against the approval of the merger should be bought by the corporation.

There are also enforcement-policy statements that guide states in analyzing mergers and acquisitions. These guidelines are issued by the U.S. Department of Justice (1992) and are also used by the antitrust enforcement agencies to analyze the proposed merger transactions. The Department of Justice (1992) maintains that horizontal mergers and acquisitions are generally very beneficial to consumers. To attempt to identify any potential antitrust issues, the government will ask a few questions during the process of analyzing a merger. They will try to find out whether the merger will produce a concentrated market or will lead to an adverse competitive environment? Will the merger aid or prevent healthy competition? Will the assets of a failed company leave the marketplace if the merger doesn't occur?

Mergers in the Telecommunications Industry

Since the beginning of the 1980s, there have been more horizontal mergers than ever before due to favorable changes in federal laws. This followed the revocation of the antitrust laws in various states to encourage mergers and acquisitions. The most widely-publicized mergers in the United States during this period were in the telecommunication industry.

The bylaws affecting the formation of mergers or acquisitions vary from state to state in the US. These bylaws touch on many aspects of a merger or acquisition. They outline the requirements for the number of corporations that are expected to merge, the issues of foreign corporations, and whether companies within the state are allowed to merge with corporations from other states. It is not possible to cover all the bylaws of each and every state in this manual. However, we will review a large number of states on matters concerning mergers or acquisitions to give you an idea about how to review these bylaws. Some states have code sections that govern the drafting of documents used in the complex merger transactions. It is a good idea to seek legal advice from a private legal counsel. Such an expert on corporate matters can help guide you through the complexities and paperwork involved in a merger.

The law requires that all merger documents have the corporate name as it is recorded in the records kept by the Secretary of State. That means all characters, even the punctuations and the corporate ending, must match exactly. It is recommended that you always check the status of the corporation(s) that will be merged. This is necessary because the state does not allow the filling of merger documents on behalf of a forfeited corporation.

Short Form Merger

The Corporations Code in most states has a section that makes it possible for a subsidiary corporation to merger with the parent using a simplified procedure. The only condition in such a transaction is that the parent company must own 100% of the subsidiary company's shares. Such a merger can be completed by simply filing a certificate of ownership with the Secretary of State in the applicable state. Using this short form merger procedure, more than two corporations can be merged by making use of a single certificate of ownership. The only requirement is that some appropriate statements need to be added in that certificate.

On matters concerning the foreign corporations, either one or more of the subsidiaries of the parent company are permitted to be foreign corporations. Even if the parent corporation is foreign-owned, the merger will be allowed to take place if any of the subsidiary companies are headquartered in the state in question.

The Corporations Code in most states also makes it possible for a parent corporation to be acquired by a subsidiary corporation. All the legislation guiding the merger are provided in the Corporation Code. In such cases, states allow a merger where the parent corporation owns less than 100% of the subsidiary's shares, but not less than 90%. There are also additional, complex statutory requirements in such cases. Perhaps because of this, fewer filings are done this way.

Merger by Agreement of Merger

In cases where a state's corporation is the surviving company, that state's bylaws require that a copy of the agreement of merger be filed alongside with a separate officer's certificate for every board member for both the merging corporation and the surviving corporation. Additional information can be found in the state's Corporations Code. All the documents are required to be stapled together, with the agreement of merger on top, followed by the various officers' certificates. You will also be required to state the basis that you will use to convert the shares of the corporations that are merging.

Triangular Merger

A triangular merger is one where the target company is acquired by a subsidiary of the acquiring company. Such transactions are legal under the bylaws of some states. The opposite of a triangular merger is a reverse triangular merger, where the subsidiary is merged into the corporation under acquisition.

There are two additional important agreements necessary in mergers and acquisitions. These are the agreement of reorganization and the agreement of merger. The agreement of reorganization puts in writing the complete agreement of all parties to the transaction. The agreement of merger is the more important of the two documents since it is the statutory agreement that is drafted, executed and filed with the state's Secretary of State.

Filing Procedures for Mergers between Domestic and Foreign Corporations

In transactions where at least one corporation is a party to a merger and is a non-US corporation, there are three ways available for the filing for a merger in a given state. Each state's requirements are somewhat different, but most require some variation of the following:

Submission of the merger documents to meet the state law requirements. This includes the officers' certificates for the surviving foreign corporation, a copy of the agreement of merger and a certificate of ownership.

Submission of a copy that has been certified and filed in the company's foreign jurisdiction. Note that this certificate must be prepared by the public official who has the custody of the original filed document.

Submission of the counterpart of the executed document that was filed in the foreign jurisdiction. Whoever is carrying out the submission must provide proof that the document has been filed in the foreign jurisdiction.

When all parties are foreign corporations, you will be required to file a certificate of surrender of rights to transact intrastate business to be able to complete the merger transaction. This filing is done on behalf of the two disappearing foreign corporations. There usually is no charge for filing the certificate of surrender of rights.

When the survivor corporation in a merger is a foreign corporation, the merger filing is made in compliance with the laws of the foreign jurisdiction. However, the details of the merger still need to be approved by the shareholders of the disappearing company. If a surviving corporation in a merger is a foreign firm, the merger will be considered effective in the foreign jurisdiction. The only US requirement is to file in the state where you will be doing business.

Nonprofit Corporations

Some states have bylaws that govern the merger of nonprofit organizations. For example, the California Corporations

Code section 6010 clearly explains public benefit corporations. The mutual benefit corporations are contained in sections 8020. All the religious corporations are discussed under section 9640. When a merger involves a nonprofit corporation, you will need the officers' certificates, an agreement of merger specifically for the surviving organization and the documents for each of the disappearing organizations.

In a merger that involves a nonprofit organization, you must also get a written consent from the Attorney General of your state. The state's Secretary of State recommends reading the Corporation Code sections that deal with nonprofits if you propose a merger involving nonprofit organizations. This is necessary so that you'll know the legal requirements of such a merger.

All the merger documents have to be mailed to the state's Secretary of State. Each state's Secretary of State has a document filing support unit for such documents. You can also have the documents hand-delivered.

Target Company Bylaws

The surviving corporation is expected to have filed the current version of their bylaws. In a case where the bylaws have changed because of the application for a merger or acquisition, the corporation will be required to file the amended bylaws. There is no need to file new bylaws in a case where the merger or acquisition does not affect the existing bylaws.

Fees for filing a merger

It costs $100 to file a merger in most states. In addition to that fee, there is an additional, non-refundable processing fee of $15. You can also speed up the processing by hand-delivering the documents and paying an additional $15 expedite fee. Each state charges slightly different fees. The numbers used here are just for illustration purposes.

Copies

Although you'll likely wish to have a copy of the processed merger documents, most states do not have the staff and capabilities to send a return copy in the mail. However, you can request a copy of the merger documents using the business entities record order form on your state's Web site. The process is very simple. You enter the company name or corporation number at the top of the Web page and submit your request. If your corporation name doesn't appear in the search results, you will generally have to file the request in person at your statehouse or by mail.

The State of Delaware (2013) argues that a merger is allowed for domestic corporations. This state allows a merger or consolidation of two or more corporations by following the existing laws. In a merger, the participating companies are permitted to take up the identity of any of the corporations involved in the merger or form a new corporation altogether. The State of Delaware (2013) further holds that to form a merger, the boards of directors should be involved in adopting a resolution which approves their companies' participation in a merger. Such a resolution should state:

How the merger will be carried into effect

The merger's terms and conditions

Any amendments in the certificate of incorporation.

The two corporations may also decide to adopt their certificate of incorporation of the purchasing corporation in its state. The surviving organization is required to make a statement declaring that the surviving corporation's certificate of incorporation will be their own as well.

IV. RECENT SHAREHOLDER COMMUNICATIONS

Many important decisions have been made by Wolff (2009) that shareholder communications are very important during the process of mergers and acquisitions and that shareholders must always be informed on what is going on during the merger process. In the past, management boards rarely communicated with shareholders directly. Shareholders often feel that directors may have ideas which differ from those of the management staff. Because of this, shareholders need to think independently on matters which affect the performance of the company. This is a clear indicator that investor expectations have changed over time. Therefore, many boards have made it routine to discuss with shareholders all the important matters affecting the company.

Matters such as mergers and acquisitions have to be discussed with the investors in mind. They will ultimately have to be convinced that the merger is worthwhile. The shareholders have to be treated just like any other stakeholder. A systematic process must be established for the sole purpose of maintaining communication with shareholders. In fact, the board should have a well-established shareholder communications policy and a method of dealing with inbound communication and inquiries from shareholders already in place.

The shareholders must be informed on matters of interest, such as CEO evaluation and succession, corporate strategy, executive compensation, director nominations and board structure after the merger and acquisition process. It is a good practice to meet with the shareholders and discuss their proposals before filing a bid. This is the right time to dispute the claims of investors who are against the merger and acquisition. This is a good way for the company to prevent the spread of wrong information that could upset the annual general meeting.

The directors who meet with shareholders should be thoroughly prepared. They must have a proper understanding of all the issues facing the company and be able to anticipate and be able to answer the most likely shareholder questions. Directors should never to be caught off-guard by shareholder questions because such a scenario will usually negatively impact their credibility.

When discussing the important issues on mergers and acquisitions, a director must develop the skill of talking face-to-face with shareholders. To do this, a director should answer their questions appropriately while remaining within the Regulation Fair Disclosure boundaries. To achieve this, it's a good idea for directors to take a training course in shareholder communication.

The directors also need to stay informed on all aspects of their company. The pre-meeting board package plays a key role in informing the directors by giving them a detailed analysis of the company shareholder base as well as the most recent changes in company ownership and topics that are of key interest to the shareholders. To make the most of director shareholder communications, it makes sense to design a way for shareholders to provide feedback and to track all the reports stemming from the original communication. The company should regularly review such reports and incorporate them in their daily company operations.

According to Davy et al. (1989), for communication to be effective, the following steps must be followed:

The information must be communicated in a timely manner.

The information should be treated as credible by the employees.

There is need to repeat the information in a large number of media outlets.

The information should be as comprehensive as possible.

The responsible officials must communicate their reasons for initiating organizational changes.

The framework for company-shareholder communications needs to be laid out for the entire timeframe from the proposal of the merger until the transaction is finalized.

During the merger and acquisition period, the company will be expected to communicate with the shareholders on a regular basis. This is one of the best ways to help the shareholders understand company policies. This is the time when transparency and accountability are particularly valued by shareholders. Being open with shareholders can yield many benefits. An open and forthcoming company is also valued by media and the community in general. Good and timely communication can have powerful effects on corporate culture and change, especially when it is done properly.

V. CERTIFICATES OF OPERATING AUTHORIZATION

There are many certificates of operating authorization. The notification of states that a merger involving a licensed company is taking place is governed by the Corporate Amendments Application Section VII. This section calls for submitting information about any change in the structure of a surviving corporation because of a merger or acquisition. All certificates of authority for non-surviving companies are surrendered to the appropriate states. The corporations are required to pay a filing fee set by the state.

Certificate of Incorporation

This key document is produced in connection with a venture capital investment portfolio. The certificate is used to establish the privileges, rights, preferences as well and restrictions of each class of stock offered by the corporation. Some organizations have a certificate of incorporation with a "non impairment" clause. This is a general and broad provision that helps in preventing the corporation from failing to act or acting in way that is likely to circumvent the specific and express sections of the certificate of incorporation. However, there are some instances where this provision can be very dangerous to the corporation and the majority shareholders. A good example is where a group of unsatisfied minority shareholders claim that violations have been made. This can easily happen in a case where there are no provisions in the certificate of incorporation to offer protection.

During a merger or acquisition, the buyer should also check the pay-to-play provision, if applicable. This is a provision that guides management on how to handle preferred stock investors when they fail to invest in future financing as expected. Some of the remedies offered for such failure include converting their shares into common stock.

The certificate of incorporation also has a choice of jurisdiction provision. This is a simple form used by the portfolio company. Many companies prefer Delaware as their choice jurisdiction for a number of reasons, such as: Delaware corporation law is frequently updated to incorporate new business and legal decisions, Delaware's case law is well developed, and Delaware has a Court of Chancery where the presiding judges are experts in business law issues. Delaware's Court of Chancery is one of the leading business courts in the U.S. In addition, the office of Delaware's Secretary of State is quite user-friendly. The filings of business documents there are done in a prompt manner. Note: a corporation may be located in another state, such as California, but still incorporated in Delaware.

When filing the certificate of incorporation, if there are major changes to the existing corporation, make sure you file the amended articles also. However, if the most-recently-filed are still accurate, you don't have to file a new articles with the certificate of incorporation. You merely have to state that the current articles are already filed in the appropriate state.

Minimum Capital and Surplus Requirements

You'll also need to file documents stating that even after the merger or acquisition, the applicant will meet the minimum capital required by the state. If that is not the case, the surviving organization will be required to make the necessary amendments to the certificate of authority. In this case, the state requires the corporation to submit a statement explaining the lack of capital. This certificate gives the corporation in question the authority to transact. The level of surplus is usually determined after a thorough scrutiny of the combined company's inventory and financial status.

The Statutory Deposit Requirement

Should the surviving corporation need to modify the filed documents after a merger, the company will need to pay a minimum deposit as required by their certificate of autho-rization. This condition mostly applies to companies in the insurance and banking industries.

VI. MINUTES OF BOARD AND OTHER MEETINGS

It is a good idea to request for the records containing the minutes of board meetings. These minutes should be ac-companied by a report from the chairman presiding over the meeting.

The report should clearly indicate the number of people who attended the meeting, the number of persons who voted in proxy and in person, the value of shares and the number of votes cast in favor or against of the merger resolution, ac-cording to Board Source (2007).

In the case of a non-profit board, meetings are set up to discuss business issues and/or address the important deci-sions affecting the organization. According to Board Source (2007), the board of directors works with the chief executive and other senior staff. The perusal of these meeting minutes is therefore necessary so that all senior executives are kept apprised of what's happening in the company or organiza-tion.

3
ISSUED SECURITIES

a. Not only is the current ownership important, but due diligence must include analysis of any and all warrants, options and other instruments that may become due during or because of any transaction. Items to check include:

I. COPIES OF STOCK CERTIFICATES

According to the Virginia State Corporation Commission (2013), in the Commonwealth of Virginia, the Clerk's office is responsible for providing both certified and non-certified copies of all business documents. This office is also responsible for offering the certificate of fact and of good standing and plays a key role in handling mergers. Company owners and other stakeholders should request copies of certified and uncertified stock certificates from this office (or the corresponding one in your state.)

The copies of stock certificates should be surrendered to the company for payment to shareholders who want to depart due to the merger process. There are some general requirements for this process that we are going to highlight here.

Such payments to shareholders must be made within 30 days of the demand for payment being made. The shares should be bought at a fair price plus any and all accrued interest. This procedure is enforced by the district court with jurisdiction over the state where the corporation is headquartered. Such payments must be accompanied by the corporation's financial documents, such as a balance sheet. This should be the most recent available and not older than 16 months. Also required to accompany shareholder payment is an income statement for that fiscal year, a statement showing any change in shareholder equity and the most recent quarterly financial statement.

According to the Delaware Secretary of State (2013), companies should never leave matters of converting or cancelling shares outstanding. All the copies of stock certificates must be converted into shares of the surviving corporation or the buyer or other securities. In some cases, the copies of stock certificates can also be cancelled. The holders of such copies receive property, cash payments, securities or rights of another corporation.

The committee responsible for the merger can decide to pay in cash instead of the recognition of fractional shares, rights or interests. All these agreements should be adopted by the committee responsible for facilitating the merger.

II. COPIES OF WARRANTS

Warranties are very important because they play three important roles during the merger or acquisition. According to McNeill et al (2000), warranties help the buyer to understand the target company and to conduct its due diligence. Secondly, the warranties make it possible for the buyer to refuse to close the deal if the warranties are in effect at closing time. Finally, the warranties make it possible for the buyer to be compensated for damages in the event that something in the filing proves to be false.

III. COPIES OF OPTIONS

According to McNeill et al (2000), there are two ways to deal with copies of options. You can either cash the options out or you can assume them. It is a good idea to first read the agreements and the terms of the equity plan in the options copies before deciding. Remember: you are not tied to those agreements. The two parties in the merger or acquisition can negotiate a different way of treating the equity other than that what is indicated on the options. In some cases, modifying these terms will require the consent of the optionees.

Cashout

A cashout occurs when the option copies are cancelled and payment made for the aggregate spread on those options. Spread is the difference between aggregate deal price and the aggregate exercise price. According to McNeill et al (2000), there are some cases where the optionees are paid a premium price to compensate them for the lost opportunity. The cashout option is popular with both buyers and option-ees.

IV. STOCK REGISTER

It is essential to understand what a stock register is and how to check it during a merger or acquisition process. According to Smith (2013), a stock register is a comprehensive database that is compiled and maintained by a company so they can track the stock issued by the company. The register includes the names of all shareholders. An accurate stock register is required for all publicly-traded companies

A stock register is very useful to the merger committee. Among the data listed on the register is information about buybacks, stock issues and retirements. It is a good idea for the companies to know how many shares each shareholder has.

According to Smith (2013), accurate information about shareholders, including names, par value and shareholders' address at the time they purchased the shares is recorded in the stock register. The dates that the shares were issued and purchased are clearly indicated. This is a good way for the company to be able to track its shares over a long period of time.

The stock register is also useful in verifying claims when stock certificates are lost and subsequently need to be replaced. In addition, the stock register is used to update owner information when stock is sold and transferred. It is a good idea to designate specific employees to maintain this register.

The people who hold the company stocks are charged with keeping the stock register up-to-date. When stockholders change their addresses, the new information must be added so they can receive their dividends. The merger committee should check to see that the stock register is well-maintained. If it is not, later verification of stock ownership will likely be very time consuming. In addition to its business role, the stock register acts as a great resource for the history of the company. It is common for historians to look at the share certificates and old stock certificates in order to learn about the broader industry.

V. SHARES ISSUED AND WHEN

The information on shares issued and when, is readily available in the stock register. There are several different types of shares: common shares, bonus shares, debenture shares, deferred shares and preferred shares. According to Shelly et al (1997), shares make up the owners' equity in the company. The various shares offered by a company and the dates they were issued should be listed. Below are some of the most common types of shares:

Preferred Shares

Preferred shares are those shares which are given preference in case of repayment of capital during the winding up of a company. The investors who hold preferred shares received a fixed rate of dividend.

There are more than one type of preferred shares:

Cumulative Preferred Shares

When a company doesn't make enough profits in a given year, the preferred shares will not be paid for that year. Those unpaid dividends are allowed to accumulate and must be paid in subsequent financial years. Only after these outstanding dividends have been paid do the quality shareholders get paid.

Non-cumulative Preferred Shares

The holders of these shares enjoy a preferential right by getting their dividends before those of common shareholders. According to Shelly et al (1997), if the company fails to make a profit in a given year, the non-cumulative do not get any dividends and they will not be paid in subsequent periods.

Redeemable Preferred Shares

It should be clear that the capital raised by shareholders cannot be repaid by the company except under certain conditions. Despite that, the capital raised using redeemable preferred shares is subject to being repaid after the predetermined period, whether or not the company is dissolved.

Participating and Non-participating Preferred Shares

Participating preferred shares are shares that allow the shareholder a portion of the excess company profit in addition to dividends. In this case, the excess profits are shared among the participating preference shareholders and the equity shareholders. Non-participating preferred shareholders do not gain from excess profits and are simply paid dividends. *Equity Shares*

Holders of equity shares get dividends and repayment of capital after the preferred shareholders have been paid. Equity shareholders are not subject to the fixed rate of dividend. Their rate of dividend varies from time to time. The directors set the rate at which dividends are paid. When there are large profits, the rate may be more than what the preferred shareholders get for their shares. However, equity shareholders are sometimes paid no dividends when the company fails to make a profit.

VI. HOLDINGS BY PERCENTAGE

The merger committee should investigate who owns what percentage of shares in the target company. This is a very important step in sorting out ownership of the company.

Those shareholders are able to swap their shares for the surviving corporation or can choose to sell their shares to the purchasing company, if they are not interested.. You can get the holdings percentages from the ownership statistics supplied by the target company. According to BP (2011), most companies do all they can to make sure that they have an updated record of shareholder percentages. They achieve that by using the year-end share register. Pay particular attention to the larger stockholders, such brokerages, custodians, market markers, stock lending institutions and foreign depositary receipt arbitrage, among others. BP (2011) further maintains that there will likely be some shares that large target companies will be unable to identify. These shares are recorded under miscellaneous. These include shares that are awaiting confirmation of holder's identity and the nature of the holders' interest in the company.

The table below is an illustration of holdings by percentage for British Petroleum (BP)

Register of Membership holding BP ordinary shares as at 31 December, 2011.

Range of Holdings	Number of Shareholders	Percentage of Total Shareholders	Percentage of Total Share capital
1-200	59,824	19.65	0.02
201-1,000	112,279	36.87	0.31
1,001-10,000	119,628	39.28	1.88
100,001-100,000	11,107	3.65	1.17
100,001-1,000,000	923	0.30	1.81
Over 1,000,000	755	0.25	94.81
	304,516	100.00	100.00

It is crucial to have an understanding of stock ownership figures. That is the best way for the merger committee to get the complete picture of who owns what in the target company and how best to compensate them for their shares. Such a table will also give the committee an idea of recent trends in shares that are held by institutions and those held by individual shareholders. The statement of stock ownership is the most important document the committee can use to achieve its goals. This standardized document shows the volume of all outstanding shares, the top ten shareholders, the ownership of mutual funds and the float and insider share holdings. We will highlight share holdings of major groups.

Institutional Share Holding

The institutional share ownership is the percentage of shares which are issued by the target company and owned by other institutions. There are many institutions that might be interested in holding shares from other companies. These organizations include investment management firms, asset management firms and research companies as well as fidelity management firms.

There are a number of subcategories of institutional ownership shares. These are as listed below:

Mutual Fund Ownership: This is the percentage of shares which are outstanding and held by institutions that invest in mutual funds.

Top Ten Institutions: This is the percentage of shares which are held by the leading ten companies in terms of share ownership.

Insider Ownership

Insider stock ownership usually comprises about 5% of all shares issued by the target company. The merger committee should pay particular attention to this type of share holding. Keep in mind that owning a five percent stake in a company can be very significant if you are dealing with a large organization. In fact, many larger companies do not have shareholders with this large an interest. Although it is rare, some corporations do have such shareholders. For example, Microsoft founder Bill Gates owns more than 10% of his company's outstanding shares. In addition, Warren Buffet's Berkshire Hathaway investment firm owns approximately 8% of Coca Cola's outstanding shares. That is what is meant by the insider ownership.

Stock Float

We can also describe share holding by using the term "float." The float is the portion of outstanding shares that are not owned by the insiders of a company.

You can calculate float as shown below:

Float % = (shares outstanding – shares owned by insiders) / shares outstanding

The merger committee, according to Money-Zine (2012), should aim at getting the most detailed information available. That means finding the names of institutions and individuals as well as mutual funds and their stock positions in the target company.

Illustration of Stock Holding

As of December 31, 2005, 997,328 shares of Microsoft were owned by Bill Gates. These shares had a market value of $26 billion, nearly 9.8% of all outstanding shares of that corporation.

The merger committee should also investigate any changes in share holding over the previous three months. Using the Microsoft example, we'll illustrate what is to be done at this stage.

Check the table below for guidance:

	Shares Held	Change in Shares	Change %	Outstanding %	Port. %
Fidelity Management & Research	283,076,978	-32,393,042	-10.0	2.7	1.4
Capital Research & Management	382,176,615	13,786,330	4.0	3.6	2.1
Barclays Global Investors International	415,122,280	-9,265,350	-2.0	4.0	1.8

From the above table, you can see that in the last three months more than nine million shares were sold by Barclays, approximately two percent of their total holding. You can also see that Barclays owns four percent of all outstanding Microsoft shares and that Microsoft shares make up approximately 1.8% of their total portfolio.

The Stock Ownership Activity

This is a summary of share holding for all the investment community. The merger committee should come up with a similar table outlining all the necessary stock information.

A sample of the table mentioned above is given below, using actual information on Microsoft as our example:

Microsoft Ownership Records (5/23/2006)	Holders	Shares
Total Positions	1,621	5,812,598,184
New Positions	88	133,568,393
Sold out positions	57	-27,854,261
Buyers	637	434,875,280
Sellers	858	-382,921,952
Net Position Change	-221	52,163,332

Explaining terms used in the table above:

Buyers: The number of institutional owners purchasing shares and the number of shares that they have bought.

New Positions: The number of new institutions buying the corporation stock as well as the number of shares that they own.

Total Positions: The sum of all institutions as well as the number of shares that are bought by those institutions.

Sellers: The numbers of institutional owners selling shares of the corporation and the number shares they are selling.

Sold out positions: These are the number of shares that are sold by the institutions that are selling all their shares.

Further Interpretation of Stock Ownership Information

According to Pushparaj (2012), there are a number of reasons why institutions buy and sell shares of a corporation. Institutional investors tend to take advantage of the short-term inefficiencies in the marketplace. This can affect their stock holdings by a wide margin. This practice is called stock arbitrage.

According to Money-Zine (2012), the merger committee should use the stock ownership information to supplement the effects that institutional shareholders can have on price of the shares. There are some huge institutions that hold a substantial number of shares, which if sold, could adversely affect the value of the corporation. Such transactions can have an effect of moving the prices dramatically. When the merger committee makes its stock analysis, management will be able to predict the consequences of such large stock movements. The committee can further learn if the target company's stock is held by institutional shareholders, the price of this company might be very volatile. This issue must be factored into the merger analysis.

VII. OUTSTANDING PREFERRED STOCK

What is Preferred Stock?

The preferred stocks are also known by other names, such as preference shares or preferred shares. This is a type of security used as equity. According to Shelly (1997), the outstanding preferred stocks are those stocks that have not been paid from the previous periods. The preferred stock works both as a debt and an equity instrument. Preferred stock ranks higher than common stock. On the other hand, it is ranked lower than bonds when it comes to claims. There are no voting rights attached to the preferred stock. They do carry a dividend, and these dividends are paid before those to common stockholders in a liquidation process. Preferred stock has its terms stated in a document called the certificate of designation. Preferred stock is similar to bond issues in that they are both rated by leading credit-rating companies. Preferred stock issues are usually rated a bit lower than bond issues from the same company.

Features of Preferred Stock

Shelly (1997) also maintains that preferred stock is a special class of shares that have a number of features not be found in common stock. Such features of preferred stock include no voting rights, more preferred than common stock, preference when paying dividends and being callable at the preference of the company.

With preferred stock, there is no assurance of dividends being paid. However, the company does have an obligation to pay stated dividends to preferred shareholders before paying common stockholders.

The merger committee should also investigate whether the company's preferred stock is cumulative or non-cumulative, according to Shelly (1997). Cumulative preferred stock dictates that if the company fails to pay the dividends at the stated rate, it must do so at a later date, meaning the dividends will accumulate over time. Some companies make dividend payments on a quarterly, semi-annual or annual basis. The merger committee needs to decide on when and how the outstanding preferred stock dividends will be paid. In the USA, the dividends on preferred stock are taxable.

Users of Preferred Stocks

Preferred stocks are very common among investors. It is important for investors to understand the benefits of different types of shares. Common shares are good when you want to have some control over the affairs of the company. On the other hand, preferred stocks only serve the company's financial interest. They do not offer investors any voting rights. The merger committee should learn how to transfer the preferred and other types of shares or even buy them outright from the shareholders. Preferred stockholders can continue to own such shares in the resulting company after the merger, or if they are not interested, they can sell the shares to the buyer of the target company.

Shelly (1997) advises that the US government has laws and regulations that oversee the issuance and exchanges of various types of shares. Some companies issue several classes of preferred stock. That is made possible in numerous rounds of financing where each round is tied to a separate class of preferred stock. These result in shares known as series A preferred, series B preferred and finally common stock.

In the United States, there are two types of preferred stocks--convertible and preferred preference. Preferred stockholders are paid a predetermined rate of interest for the shares that they hold.

Note: there are a number of income tax benefits for companies that invest in preferred stocks in the U.S. Other benefits of preferred stocks include higher yields, ranking ahead of common stock and tax advantages.

VIII. ANY APPLICABLE COVENANTS

According to Hirschfeld (2010), business restrictive covenants should not appear in post-deal employment agreements. Those covenants should instead be tied to some particular terms of the purchase agreement. Enough research should be done to find out whether to tie the covenants to specific parts of the deal.

Make a good use of forfeiture provisions plus injunctive relief. There are a number of restrictive covenants that are executed during the time of the transaction. In this case, you must keep in mind that your decisions will vary depending on your state and jurisdiction.

IX. OUTSTANDING WARRANTS, OPTIONS AND OTHER SECURITIES

According to Wilson et al (2009), a stock option is defined as a contract between two people to provide the holder the right to sell or buy an outstanding stock at a specific date at a specific price. Stock options are usually offered when people expect that a stock will go up or down. This greatly depends on the option type. A good example of using a stock option is when a stock currently trading at $50 is expected to rise to $60 within the next few days. The goal is to buy the call option now and sell it in the next few weeks when the trading price reaches $60. That way you will make a profit of $10 per share. These options are bought and sold along with stocks at the securities exchange.

A stock warrant is similar to a stock option. This instrument gives you the right to own a company's stock at a particular price. There are two main ways that a stock warrant differs from an option:

New shares are issued by the company for the main purpose of a transaction. The stock warrant is usually issued directly by the corporation unlike a stock option. On exercising a stock option, the shares change hands from one investor to the other. When you exercise a stock warrant, the shares that fulfill the given obligation are never received from investor. Instead they are issued by the company.

A stock warrant is always issued by the company itself.

Stock warranties are issued by companies in order to raise money. The buying and selling of stock options makes it possible for the company that owns stock never to receive any cash from the transactions. On the other hand, a stock warrant is the best way for the company to raise money through stocks or equity. Actually, a stock warrant is a smart way to claim ownership of a company. Wilson (2009) maintains that the warrant stock is always offered at a price lower than that of the stock option. The time limit on an option is usually two or three years. On the other hand, a stock warrant can last up to 15 years. This is one reason why a stock warrant is a better long-term investment than a stock option.

Other Securities

Callable Bonds

The merger committee should clearly understand that callable bonds are those bonds which can be called by the issuer after a specific period of time. According to Spaulding (2011), there is usually a call protection period at a particular price. This is referred to as the call price. This price is usually higher than the bond's face value, especially during the initial year when the bond can actually be called. This price decreases as the time to maturity elapses. Sometimes bond issuers practice edging because they issue the callable bonds in anticipation of a future decrease in interest rates. These issuers have a duty to pay the buyer a higher coupon rate in order to compensate them for what is termed the call risk. This compensation is done by the bondholder so that the bond may be called earlier. Bonds are virtually always called when interest rates decrease. The premise is to insure that bondholders do not lose the interest they would have gotten had they held the bond to maturity. Another reason for calling bonds is because of capital appreciation due to increased bond prices. This is usually capped at the call price. The reinvestment risk dictates that a bondholder will not invest in another bond that pays an equal interest rate for an equivalent credit risk.

One question that stands out is how the bond issuer prices a callable bond. There are a lot of similarities between a straight bond and a callable bond. Straight bonds have callable options from the bondholder. Such options can be quite valuable to the issuer. That is why the issuer has an obligation to compensate the bondholder if they call the bond. Many things go into calculating the bond call option. For one thing, the call cannot be exercised until the end of the call protection period. In addition, the price paid reduces as the maturity time decreases.

Convertible Securities

According to Spaulding (2011), holders of convertible preferred stock and convertible bonds have an option of converting their securities into common stock of the issuing company. The main characteristics of the convertible securities are that they explicitly name the conversion ratio. The conversion ratio is defined as the number of shares that can be converted for every convertible security. This can be determined by using the conversion price.

The convertible price is always specified before the security is issued. In most cases, this price is higher than the market value of stock. If that were not the case, the bond buyers would almost always convert their bonds into stock, making it all but useless for a company for a company to offer such a security. The desirability of converting a convertible security depends on the current stock price.

A given stock needs to appreciate significantly before a conversion makes sense. There has to be an increase in the stock price for the call option to increase in value. The bond price moves comparatively higher as the stock price moves above the conversion price. The conversion value is always lower than the convertible bond. This is because the bond provides some protection against a decline in stock price. In a case where the stock declines far below the conversion value, the bond still maintains its value as a straight bond. Owning a stock that is protected and has a strike price in a similar way as the straight bond is like buying a convertible security. The bond price is largely determined by a stock price that is higher than the conversion price. This is because the yield-to-maturity is always lowered when the value of the bond increases.

It is difficult to calculate the value of the call feature of convertibles. This is because dividends have likely been paid before the bond is converted. In addition, the conversion price may have been raised at some point since the bond was purchased. Bear in mind that the majority of the convertibles are callable. That is why when the company issues a call on the convertible, a forced conversion results. This is even more likely to occur when the conversion price is below the stock price. In order for the bondholders to realize immediate profits, they have a full month in which to convert their stock in case the conversion price is lower than the current stock price.

Warrants

Warrants are referred by many other names, such as stock-purchase warrants or subscription warrants. These are actually call options written by a company in order to buy its common stock at a particular price. The time period for such practice is also specified. Note that there are some perpetual warrants which do not expire. In this case, the warrant buyer pays and the money goes directly to the company. It is the same case with the money paid for the purpose of exercising the warrant in order to receive company stock. According to Spaulding (2011), when the warrant is exercised, the company has an obligation to issue new stock. That actually increases the number of outstanding shares. These are recorded in the financial accounts as diluted earnings per share.

The needs of the company dictate the terms of the warrant. These are therefore never standardized like they are with listed options. Warrants are able to be adjusted for the purpose of stock splits and stock dividends. Warrants are usually issues with some attachment to the bonds. This is a powerful way to reduce dividends that must be paid to sell the securities. Note that these warrants are actually detachable and are always called detachable warrants. They can therefore be traded independently of the security attached to it.

X. OPTIONS AND OTHER EMPLOYEE BENEFITS

There are many cases when a merger brings in completely new benefits for the employees that stay with the new company. Such benefits are an important part of any employee compensation package. A merger brings unrest among employees of both companies. Among these worries is the uncertainty about the benefits, such as health insurance, pension plans and paid vacation time that they enjoyed from the old company. The purchasing company should thoroughly research the existing benefit plans so they can explain to employees how those benefits will be affected after the purchase.

The new company will also need to explain any new benefits that the employees will realize as a result of the merger or acquisition. The sale will most likely come with new health insurance providers as well as new company procedures and enrollment practices. All aspects of the new benefits should be thoroughly explained to the staff, including how they will handle health insurance deductibles for those having to switch health care providers and those employees with covered dental procedures in progress.

The new company should compare the benefit structures, labor contracts, vacation policies, benefit eligibility, retirement plans and sick plans between the new and the old company. Being well versed on the details of both the new and old benefit packages will make explaining the new package to employees and having them accept it much easier.

Payroll Process

In addition to enrolling all acquired employees in the new benefit plans, it is also important to add them to the payroll system. This generally requires a good amount of new-hire paperwork, with employees needing to fill out new W-4 forms so that the taxes can be deducted from their wages. Employees who use direct deposit will need to complete additional paperwork.

Employee Stock Options

There are four events necessary for awarding employee stock options:

Granting of the stock option

Vesting of the option

Exercising of the option

Lapse of the option

On the date the option is granted, employees are allowed to exercise that option at the option price. The elapse date is defined as the date on which the option expires.

The Call Option

The call option is usually stated at the grant date. The exercise price for employees is always set below the market price. The merger committee will find such options are treated by accounting as compensation. Such compensation is included in the income statement over the vesting period.

Despite the fact that most options are offered at a price less than the market price, many options are exercised "at the money," where the market price is equal to the exercise price. This happens when the market price increases over time. When options are exercised "at the money," there is no need to record compensation expense. When options are offered, it is treated as the distribution of company wealth amongst the employees. This is usually done at the expense of the shareholders. That is explained through showing that the value of shares held by such shareholders must drop in order to show the dilution of their equity. GAAP regulations treat this transaction in two ways.

For one thing, such stock options are operational transactions, since they are part of employees' compensation packages. Secondly, they are financing transactions, since they raise cash for the target company.

When the target company offers stock at a price lower than the market price, they are required to give those employees cash for the difference so that they can be in a position to buy the shares.

Note that the target company gets a tax deduction as a result for this portion of the expense incurred by employees exercising their options. That is why the accounting records should always recognize the expense.

In case of a loss from exercise of options, the target company should report such a loss. This actually is a legitimate loss. Investors are always very sensitive about expected future losses. The merger should therefore address the value of options with great care. They should therefore focus on the expected losses in future. Such an expected loss is called option overhang. This is the estimated loss if the options are sold at the current market prices.

It is a common practice for firms to use warranties and options in addition to wages or salaries, especially for top level executives. In the United States, GAAP requires the use of grant-date accounting for stock options. It is also the same case as the requirement of IFRS2, supported by International Accounting Standards Board (IASB).

All compensation costs that are unearned are to be recorded under the grant date. This is followed by recognizing it as an expense in the income statement to be spread over the period the employee works for the company.

It is a common practice for all unearned compensation to be recorded more especially at a grant date. This is followed by recognizing the expense in the income statement. It is also a good idea to match the expense against the revenue that is produced by employees. After the grant date is over, any extra losses are recognized as losses. The following steps are needed for proper accounting of stock options.

The option value should be recognized at the grant date as a contingent liability as well as an unearned asset. These two items are then compared on the company's balance sheet. Under the FASB Statement, the amount recognized is the option value but at the grant date and called employee compensation.

In the second step, the deferred compensation is to be amortized over the period that the employee will be with the company. This is called the vesting period.

The third step involves marking the contingent liability so to market it as an option that goes into money and to reflect the value of the option overhang. The unrealized loss must be recognized from the stock options.

The liability against the share issue must be written off, but at market value and at the exercise date.

It has been noted that the employee stock options are not the only way losses can be hidden. The same thing happens with the contingent equity claims. The firm's own stock has options and call, warrants, convertible bonds, rights and finally the preferred, convertible shares. The issue or repurchase of shares at a price different from the market value happens frequently

IFRS and GAAP do not recognize the cost of financing using the convertible bonds and the convertible preferred stock.

XI. EMPLOYEE STOCK OWNERSHIP

The merger committee should find out whether the target company had a practice of issuing shares to the employees at prices lower than the market price. They should further investigate whether the difference between the market price and the issue price is treated as directed by GAAP and IFRS as compensation to the company employees. This is actually treated as an expense in the income statement.

In most cases, the employees are never granted shares. They are instead offered stock options that are followed by shares at a later date. The IFRS and GAAP are not very efficient in the reporting of share options and shareholder value.

4
FINANCIALS

a. The numbers and the care with which they are prepared say a lot about the company; be sure to check the presentation as well as the content.

b. Items to check:

I. AUDITED FINANCIALS SINCE INCEPTION

During the merger and acquisition process, the target company is required to supply complete audited financial sheets to the buyer to examine. These documents include a change of equity form, the balance sheet, a profit and loss statement and cash flow analysis, among others. These comprise the annual report as certified by an independent certified public accountant. The annual report must have a clearly-detailed analysis of business, property and financial highlights for each year. The annual report includes financial information as well as management discussion and analysis. The audit committee also gives a report. The company explains how they picked the auditors. Details of the auditors' identity and specific skills and any interaction with them are indicated in the report.

Be sure to read the disclosure of any disagreements with accounts and changes in accounting methods. Also pay attention to the quarterly reports to gain additional insight into the company's financial operations. These quarterly reports are very important because they give a clearer picture of what is happening during the year and are useful in gaining a better understanding of the target company's financial health.

The financial records will also reveal any extraordinary events, such as change of fiscal year, bankruptcy or state receivership, any amendments made to the code of ethics and any other unique event the company chooses to disclose.

II. BALANCE SHEETS

According to Evans (2000), the balance sheet may have to be analyzed over a period of six months for a merger to be successful. When the acquiring company spends between four to six months reviewing financial documents, there is a greater likelihood of arriving at a realistic value for the target company. There are a number of areas you need to focus on as you study the balance sheet. Look for those assets that have been overvalued. These are called low quality assets. You'll need to ascertain their true market values. It is also a good idea to scrutinize the company's liabilities and identify those that are understated. These can be allowances, bad debts and pensions. Again there may be some hidden liabilities, such as cases of contingencies for lawsuits that are never recorded.

The target company's inventory should be reviewed with great care so as to identify any overstated inventories. If you discover that the inventories are rising over a period of time,

that is an indicator of low market demand on rising obsolescence. It is also possible that LIFO reserves are causing a
distortion.

If the receivables are overstated, it likely means that those
receivables are not collectable. This is commonly found with
inter-company receivables.

The balance sheet should be analyzed to determine the valuation of the short-term marketable securities. In some cases,
you will discover that the target company is holding those
securities. Find out whether those securities are valued well.
In a case where the company is holding investments, check
whether they are overstated to avoid any confusion.

Intangibles

Many companies forget to properly value intangibles, such
as brand names. In most cases, it should be easy to differen-
tiate between market and book values. If you find that there
is no difference between the two, there is likely some serious
manipulation on the submitted documents.

III. CASH FLOWS

Cash flow is the movement of money into and out of a financial product or a business. The cash flow is normally measured over a specific period of time. This document can be
used in calculating other perspectives of a company's value.
The following are some of the parameters that can be determined from a cash flow statement:

The cash flow statement can be used in calculating the company's value or rate of return. This financial document is
also used in calculating the inputs in the financial models,

such as the internal rate of return as well as the net present value (NPV).

Cash flow is used in determining the liquidity problems of a business. There is a great difference between being profitable and being liquid. Some companies fail even after being very profitable due to a lack of cash.

The cash flow statement is used to measure profits where companies feel that accrual accounting does not accurately reflect their economic realities. A good example is where a company is profitable, but there is limited operational cash. This can happen when a company participates in barter trade rather than selling goods for cash. In such cases, the company will need to raise cash through the issue of shares or engaging in debt financing to cover expenses. These are some of the important issues that have to be studied by the merger committee so they can fully understand the workings of the target company.

The quality of income generated through accrual accounting can be evaluated using the cash flow statement. In a case where the net income is made up of non-cash items, that is considered low quality net income. The company's cash flow can also help with an evaluation of risks within a particular financial product. That includes evaluating default risk, matching of cash requirements and re-investment requirements.

Different users of the term cash flow use the term differently. Some either refer to cash flow to project future cash flow or past cash flow. It can also be used to describe a subset of cash flows or the total of all flows involved. Some of these subsets include free cash flow, net cash flow and operating cash flow.

The cumulative net cash of the target company over a period of time is equal to the cash balance over that same period of time. If there is an increase in cash, you'll have a positive balance. On the other hand, a decrease in cash yields a negative balance. Other areas to analyze to better understand the company's total cash flow include:

Financing Cash Flow: This is the cash received due to the issue of debt or equity. Sometimes it is paid as debt repayments, share repurchases and dividends.

Operational Cash Flow: This is the cash received or paid to support the company's business activities. This also includes changes to working capital as well as cash earnings. This must always be positive over the medium term in order for the company to remain in business.

Investment Cash Flow: This is the cash received from the sale of long-term assets.

The following are ways to improve cash flow:

Payment of Wages: Try as much as possible to pay using the stock options.

Equipment Leases: It's often more beneficial to buy equipment outright than to lease it.

Consulting Fees: These should be paid using shares from the company treasury, if possible.

Rent: Again, buying property is often more beneficial than renting.

R & D: The company can wait for the product to be tested by a start-up lab before buying the lab in an acquisition or a merger.

Interest: Issue convertible debt.

Sales: It is often a good idea to sell receivables to a collection company to get quick cash.

IV. ACCOUNTING METHODS AND PRACTICES

It is very important to understand how you are going to check the accounting practices of the target company during a merger or acquisition. There are two techniques used to account for mergers and acquisitions. The entire merger or acquisition transaction can be treated as a purchase. You will be required to restate the assets of the target company in fair market value, then get the difference between the prices paid and the fair market value. The difference should be posted to the balance sheet under goodwill.

The book values of two companies are combined after a merger or acquisition. In this case, the goodwill is not recognized. This is called pooling of interest and it is only applicable for companies that involve only stock.

Historically, when physical assets were more important, the purchase method was the most frequently-used accounting technique for mergers and acquisitions. Today, companies tend to put more value on intellectual capital and other intangible aspects of the business. That explains the increased use of the pooling of interest method. Failing to recognize intellectual assets of a company will lead to a distorted view of the company's financial health.

According to Wood and Sangster (2006), when a business is sold in a merger, the seller makes a lot of money through goodwill of the business. When a business is bought through a merger or acquisition, there is no need for the seller to re-evaluate the assets and record the updated information in his books. It will be the duty of the purchaser to record the changes in assets in the balance sheet as indicated above.

It is very important to spend enough time scrutinizing the accounting records even if they involve some investigative methods. You can even send some undercover agents to confirm the financial records that are presented to you. According to Evans (2000), things can quickly go wrong in a merger or acquisition if you do not carry out the proper due diligence. There are many real life examples where things have gone wrong in the past because of a lack of due diligence. A perfect example is the merger between CUC International and HFS Inc. This merger was announced. Then, after four months, it was discovered that there were some serious accounting irregularities. After the news was announced, the newly-formed company--Cendant--reported a loss of more than $14 billion in terms of the market value.

All the financial statements presented to the buyer by the seller must be checked for consistency and that they have been prepared in accordance with all the accepted accounting principles. All prior periods must also match with the current financial periods. The financial information should fairly represent the financial position of the target company. Be sure that the seller includes financial representations even if all the financial documents have been audited by an accounting firm of good reputation. This indicates an improved control over the key businesses of the target corporation. These accounts can be useful in decision making. The areas that need attention are exposed by management accounts. These are the documents used by buyers during mergers to reduce future uncertainties.

V. REVENUE RECOGNITION POLICIES

How to recognize revenue is one of the most complex, but important questions that face companies. The merger committee must take time to find out the revenue recognition policies of its target company. This is one of the auditing and accounting areas that involve plenty of risk. Normally, you'll find physical weaknesses when it comes to financial reporting of the internal controls. This is caused by failure of internal controls when it comes to revenue recognition.

According to PWC (2012), there are multiple solutions that companies offer to their customers. These can include performance or just delivery of a number of services and products. This normally occurs at different times and points. When contracts have numerous income generating activities, there are a number of rules that must be followed to identify revenues. Note: the rules for revenue recognition are very detailed and are changing daily. Revenue recognition is usually governed by two important bodies as listed below:

International Auditing Standards Board (IASB) and

The US Financial Accounting Standards Board (FASB)

The two bodies listed have come up with new regulations on revenue recognition policies. In case these regulations are adopted, the revenue recognition landscape will change dramatically. The PWC (2012) maintains that the benefit of the new proposed model is that it will promote consistency across many industries. Some feel that the new model is simpler. This is because the detailed rules that cover most transactions have been eliminated. They are replaced by a model that uses general principles. However, this simplicity comes with a need for disclosure as well as trade-off. Those that use this new model will need to make plenty of decisions and changes to their business practices.

The Impact of Revenue Recognition Policies

There are several reasons why revenue recognition policies are important to a large number of businesses, and such policies affect a number of areas within a company.

These policies affect the financial reporting, accounting policies, personnel (via training and education), information systems, process and controls, performance metrics and operations.

When companies adopt a new revenue reporting policy, they need time to plan and manage the impacts of this new policy .

Companies adopting the new policies should:

Ensure they have the correct documentation and other controls in place. The controls are used in supporting the document estimates. There is also a need to have proper guidance on revenues and analysis.

All the details of all transactions should be understood. The companies should strive to understand not only the current but also the future accounting models that apply to their transactions.

For companies that have international operations, they should make sure that the employees receive enough training so that they are familiar with how the GAAP are applied in the United States.

Better Understanding of the Matching Principle

The merger committee should try to understand how the target company reports revenue. Those companies that adopt the GAAP regulations apply the matching principle--when expenses are matched with the revenues. That means that the expenses and income are reported at the exact time when they are incurred and are earned. This is done even when they are no cash transactions.

A good example of the matching principle is where a company makes a sale of $50,000 within a specific financial period, but it has not yet received payment. Despite the fact that the company has not yet received the payments, the sale has to be recorded as revenue for that period. This is what is meant by matching revenues with expenses. All expenses incurred in a particular accounting period have to be matched with the revenue they generated.

When revenues are not matched with the expenses incurred during the same period, the company financial statements do not accurately reflect their true financial situation.

The merger committee should further recognize that some target companies follow the SFAS 5 revenue recognition principles. These are detailed below:

The Completion of the Earning Process

This principle means that the target company has provided all the products and services for which it is to be paid. In addition, it implies that that the company is in a position to measure all implied costs and that the company has no remaining obligations to its customers.

Payment Assurance

There must be a way to measure assets or cash. This is the money to be received for the services and goods already supplied. The likelihood of payment should be accurately accessed by the company for this principle to hold.

Net and Gross Reporting of Revenue

Under this principle, the sales and cost of goods sold are reported separately. The net revenue is then calculated by subtracting the cost of goods sold from the sales made for that particular fiscal year. In this case, only the net revenue is reported.

GAAP requires that any firm adopting the gross revenue principle for revenue reporting should be a primary party to the contract in question. The company should be in a position to take both the credit and inventory risk. Next, it should be able to choose suppliers and set its own prices.

When analyzing financial statements, the merger committee should be informed about the aggressiveness of the revenue recognition policies adopted by the company. A target company that is too aggressive in its revenue recognition policy risks overstating its revenues.

The merger committee should also be aware of any judgments and assumptions that may exist when reporting company revenues. Revenues received in advance are not recognized as revenue. These are actually treated as liabilities. There are two conditions that have to be met:

There are those revenues recognized when cash or receivables are received in exchange of services or goods. The realization of revenues is possible when the exchange is readily convertible into a claim of cash.

When goods are rendered, revenues are earned.

Revenue Recognition for Main Types of Transactions

The revenue generated from the sale of an asset that is not inventory. Recognition is done at the point of sale.

Permission to use a company's assets: revenue is recognized when assets are used or after a time limit.

Selling Inventory: revenue is recognized on the date of sale. This is also treated as the date of delivery.

Rendering Services: revenue is recognized when services are billed on completion.

Exceptions:

Revenues not recognized at sale

There are a number of exceptions when we talk about revenues from sale of inventory. The merger committee should find out whether the target company follows the principles correctly.

Returns: Companies that have a high rate of returns should recognize revenues when the right to return period expires.

Buyback agreements: This is an agreement where the company sells a product with a plan to buy it at a later date. When the buyback price covers other related costs, then no sale has taken place.

Revenues recognized before sale

Long-term contracts

This is another exception that occurs when the target company is engaged offers long-term contracts. A good example is building and construction projects. Stadiums, highways and aircraft take a long period of time to build. These kinds of projects allow the contractor to bill the client at different stages during the contract, such as after every five miles of highway are built.

The Percentage-of-completion method

This method is used when there is a contract that lays out specific payments terms. In such a case, the buyer is expected to pay the whole amount when the seller completes the project. The gross profit is recognized for each period with the corresponding costs. This is based on the progress of construction. For example, when a project is 25% complete, the builder can recognize an equivalent amount of cost and revenue. If there is a loss, that should be recognized immediately. This is because of the conservatism constraint. The calculation of percentage of completion is an accounting requirement and it helps in budget comparisons and as a precaution in controlling the cost of long-term projects.

The method that is most commonly used in calculating revenue for long-term contracts is extremely complex. There are two main methods used in calculating the completion percentage:

Finding the accumulated cost as a percentage of the total budgeted cost.

Determination of the portion of the completed deliverable as a percentage of total deliverable.

The second technique listed is very accurate, but tedious. There is a software used called ERP that can integrate Human resources, inventory and financial information. The planning and scheduling is done when all cost components are logged according to the WBS elements.

When the percentage-of-completion is not complicated, you are advised to make use of the completed-contract method. This is applicable for those projects that involve great risks. Gross profit, costs and methods are recognized after the project is completed successfully. That means that if a company is working on a single project, its income statement will show zero in revenues as well as zero construction costs until the fiscal year ends. Despite that requirement, the expected loss should be recognized accordingly.

Completion of production basis

Completion of production basis is another accounting method that recognizes revenue even in a case where a sale was made. That applies most often to minerals and agricultural products. The method is most commonly used when there is a ready market for the products. In such markets, you are assured of a minimum price. In addition, there are a few distribution and selling costs involved.

Revenues recognized after Sale

In some cases, there is a high level of risk involved in collecting receivables. Where there is a high level of risk associated with collecting a debt, then the company must recognize the debt. There are three accounting methods that apply in such situations:

Deposit Method:

In this method, the company receives cash before the transfer of ownership is complete. In such a case, the revenue cannot yet be recognized. This is because the rewards and risks of ownership have not been fully transferred to the buyer.

Installment sales method:

This method makes it possible to recognize income immediately after the sale by noting the proportion of gross profit and the cash collected. All unearned income is deferred and possibly recognized at a later date when the cash is collected.

Cost Recovery Method:

This method is used in cases where there is a high probability that payments will remain uncollected. Therefore, no profit is recognized until the cash collected more than covers the cost of the products sold. For example, a company that sold a machine worth $10,000 for a price of $15,000 can start recording profit only when it receives more than $10,000.

VI. MANAGEMENT ACCOUNTS

Management accounts can give buyers a good look at the performance of the business. Such management accounts provide financial information on the areas where the business is performing well as well as those areas where it is underperforming. These underperforming areas are the ones that need extra attention from the buyers or company owners. During the merger, buyers should ask to examine the management accounts so they can identify those areas that need attention before it is too late.

Make sure that the management accounts are prepared by an experienced accountant and that they are presented in a proper format. The numbers presented in these management accounts should be easy to understand. This is important because a large number of business managers and owners do not have extensive financial background. If this is the case, the accountant can act as a financial advisor to the prospective buyer.

There are three main financial reports which are provided under the management accounts:

Balance Sheet

Profit & Loss Statement

Cash Flow Statement

There may also be additional reports included, such as accounts receivable report, a customer list, a list of suppliers, an accounts payable report and a margin and sales analysis.

The wage analysis report may also be provided with other management accounts. The buyer during a merger should look closely at all of the salient features in the management accounts.

According to Independent Focus (2012), a large number of business organizations limit their accounting activities to tax returns, bookkeeping and dealing with debtors and creditors. As you look at these accounts, you will be able to learn things like how the company performance compares with the forecasts or budgets. You will likely be able to also forecast cash flow for the next few months. These management accounts are therefore critical for analyzing the target company.

VII. BUDGETS AND PROJECTIONS

Projections must support the proposed operating plan. Some typical components include of these projections include delegated function arrangements. Do not forget to outline assumptions used in the projections in your new operating plan.

Financial Projections

Many managers of big corporations will tell you that in order to succeed in business, you need to understand the numbers. Financial projections are directly related to the future. This is where they differ from accounting data (which is a record of past data.) Projections are used to show how the business can be profitable. The assumptions used are based in the market price, data, costs and other parameters.

Financial projections are also used to develop data that can be used in making financial judgments. Many components make up financial projections, such as return on equity, financing methods to be used, return on investments, growth patterns and the required investment. Projections should always be constructed to cover reasonable timeframes. The exact period depends on your type of business.

Assumptions make up an important part of financial projections. Uncovering the cost of production and the amount to be produced are some of the issues that are based on assumptions. The amount that customers are willing to pay for the products and the estimated costs that will face the company are just two examples of such assumptions. Assumptions also include market conditions. This is made possible using market analysis. Such assumptions make it possible for the company management to make particular statements about prices. According to Duermyer (2012), financial projections help in specifying and articulating assumptions that might later be challenged. Assumptions made should always be tested against the real conditions in the industry to gauge accuracy.

When preparing projections, the state of the industry should also be analyzed well. Industry production costs can be projected. This helps in making assumptions about the specific business production cost. It is generally held that many financial projections are presented as if they are accounting information. That is not the case. Projections contain information about the future while accounting deals with historic events. According to Duermyer (2012), financial projections are useful in getting a overview of a company. Most businesses make future projections so they can allocate resources accordingly.

Using a spreadsheet is the most appropriate way to prepare financial projections because it provides plenty of flexibility. According to Duermyer (2012), a financial projection should start with a table that clearly defines all assumptions and how they are to be used to determine projected sales, marketing costs, prices, equity, long-term debt, wages, equipment productivity, interest rates and number of employees, among other factors. The merger committee determines whether the assumptions table has any relation to the income statement, balance sheet and/or other cash flow statements. The merger committee should also look at the worksheets to ensure that they include all the necessary information. The information on those sheets should be compared to those related to the average and mean assumptions. Using a spreadsheet also allows financial analysts to make necessary changes quickly.

A large number of software programs can be used in generating financial projections. Such programs should be evaluated by the committee. In addition to getting the results as financial statements and pre-formatted tables, software can generate graphs and other visible reports. Some companies use online tools to come up with financial projections.

Financial projections need to be as accurate as possible. The merger committee should therefore do its best to determine whether the projections are accurate by reviewing previous projections and assumptions. Financial projections should be in line with the performance of similar businesses in the industry. Projections should be made for every step, such as supply of inputs, outbound logistics, processing and marketing. The merger committee should read all the assumptions that support financial projections to determine their implications for the business as a whole.

It is a good idea to present financial projections on a monthly or quarterly basis as well as an annual one because of seasonal fluctuations in sales. This will allow for short-term goals as well as long-term projections. At this point, the merger committee should take a closer look at the target company's cash flow. This is a prime indicator of whether the company will succeed in the long run. They should also look at the annual rate of return on investment. The purchasing company should know the internal rate of return of the target company. In addition, the merger committee should access the net present value (NPV) of the company, a prime determinant of the company's worth. The committee should further compare the expected return on sales and other ratios to get an idea of the company's profitability and how it compares with its competitors.

Budget Projections

Budget projections are usually submitted quarterly. The merger committee should look to these documents for indications of the target company's yearly goals. Budgets are usually accompanied by an explanation as well as a contingency plan. The explanation should address any drastic changes in the budget from previous quarters. Budget projections are very important because they enable future budget revisions to accommodate unbudgeted expenses.

Budgets are a good way to monitor company growth. This will give you a picture of where company money is being spent and which areas of the target business are exceeding the budget projections. Budgets are also usually prepared for specific business departments, such as marketing, promotion or IT.

A reasonable sales projection is needed to prepare an accurate budget. The merger committee should check that the numbers presented in the budget are based in fact. The purchasing company will benefit immensely from accurate budget projections.

The merger committee should evaluate the number of employees needed to run the company and whether these employees are being paid at or above the market rate. Information on average salaries can be obtained from the US Bureau of Labor Statistics. Obviously, offering competitive salaries makes it easier to attract and keep competent workers. Any budget needs to include information on salaries.

The budget also needs to include insurance, taxes and rent. Some budget items are fixed, such as rent. Others are able to be adjusted, such as the cost of marketing. After the merger, there are some sections of the budget which will likely be adjusted.

VIII. BUSINESS PLAN

According to Entrepreneur (2013), when a surviving company's business plan is not changed after the merger, a statement has to be issued to that effect. If there are changes to be made on the business plan, the corporation has to submit a plan of operation. Such a plan needs to include two important aspects of the business: pro-forma financial projections and a narrative that briefly supports the application.

IX. ACCOUNTS RECEIVABLE ANALYSIS

Accounts receivable are amounts that are owed to a business by its customers. The majority of these records consist of outstanding invoiced amounts. The merger committee should be prepared to spend time analyzing these accounts receivables and matching them to invoices. That is the only way through which you can understand the cash flow involved.

There are accounting software packages that print an accounts receivable aging report, one of the easiest methods of analyzing accounts receivables. Such software makes these numbers easier to understand by dividing the accounts receivables into groups, usually set to reflect company billing terms. The most commonly-used time groups are 0-30 days old, 31 – 60 days, 61-90 days old and those over 90 days old. The merger committee should be concerned if most of the accounts receivables are older than 30 days.

There are a number of factors to look for as you carry out the accounts receivable analysis.

Analyzing the bucket size

Thoroughly analyze the time bucket size. Make sure that this time bucket size is corresponding to the credit terms followed by the company.

Consider the distance from the billing date

Many large companies invoice all of their companies at the end of the month. That means that if the aging report is run a couple of days later, it will likely show many outstanding accounts receivable from the previous month, those receivables that were just billed. Such a scenario doesn't usually mean that the accounts receivable are in a bad condition.

Check the individual credit terms

Check out whether some customers have been granted extended credit. They will usually only affect a few invoices. In cases of extended credit, the transactions may appear to be overdue when they are not.

The second tool to use for accounts receivable analysis is called the trend line. At the end of each month, the merger committee should plot the total accounts receivable. The resulting graph can be used in to predict future accounts receivable. This tool is particularly well-suited to analyzing businesses with highly seasonal sales.

According to Accounting Tools (2012), using trend line analysis is very useful in comparing the percentage of bad debts over time. If you find this percentage holding steady over time, it makes sense to tighten the credit terms offered to the customers.

There are a few things that can be pointed out about using trend line analysis:

Change in Product lines: When a company deletes or adds to its product mix or business line, it is likely to cause a change in the accounts receivable trend line.

Credit Policy Changes: Any changes in the target company's credit policy can also lead to changes in bad debt and accounts receivable totals.

The third type of accounts receivable analysis is called the ratio analysis. This method uses the collection period to measure receivables by measuring the average length of time it takes a customer to pay their invoice. Here is the formula used to get the ratio:

Average Accounts Receivable/ (Annual Sales/365 Days)

The following is an example of using ratio analysis:

If the company has an average of $500,000 in accounts receivables over a specific period, and annual sales are $3,650,000, we can calculate the accounts receivable collection period as follows:

$500,000 (Accounts Receivable) / ($3,650,000/365 Days) = 50 days as collection period.

This calculation only gives us the debt collection period. From just this figure, there is no way of knowing whether that is a good or bad thing. We need also to know the duration of the credit terms.

It is important to note that the best way to analyze accounts receivable is to use a combination of all the three techniques discussed above. By using the accounts receivable collection period, you gain a general idea about the ability of the target company to collect its debts. From the analysis of the aging report, you'll learn about specific invoices that are creating collection problems. Finally, by using trend analysis, you'll see how problems with receivables have varied over time.

Additional types of analysis

There is an additional analysis tool that is useful in scrutinizing accounts receivable. This is the trend line that outlines the proportion of customer sales for which payment is collected at the time of the sale. Look particularly at the type of payment used and how a shift away (or towards) up-front payments affects the company's financial health.

X. ACCOUNTS PAYABLE ANALYSIS

The merger committee should learn to perform some basic analysis on accounts payable in order to have a better understanding of the business as a whole and to understand how payments are made to creditors. Other names for accounts payable include trade creditors, A/P or AP. These are the amounts that the company has to pay the suppliers for the goods or services supplied to the company. The payable accounts are initiated when the company gets credit from a supplier. According to Bilson (2010), accounts payable make up part of the company's liabilities and are reported to that effect in the financial reports.

It is a good business practice for a company to pay its accounts payable in a timely manner. Such an action helps a lot in monitoring the cash outflow in the business cash account. Many companies use trend analysis to track accounts payable. To use trend analysis effectively, you will need to use information from a variety of different sources, such as competitors, business, industry averages and peer companies. Checking industry benchmarks can also be helpful. You should be able to see trend variations, depending on the nature of the company's business.

The information gained through trend analysis can be used in evaluating the company's performance. This is a good indicator of how efficiently the company handles its payments. According to Bilson (2010), the merger committee should study the accounts payable over a period of two to five years.

Sample Analysis of Accounts Payable

In analyzing accounts payable, start by comparing purchases made from major company suppliers over previous periods. Next, compare other related payments between current and previous periods. You will also need to compare current and prior year creditor reports. Take into account write-offs and other related expenses that are stated as a percentage of accounts payable. Any non-recurring items may cause a distortion in this comparison. Some of the distortions may be caused by accounting changes, acquisitions of new business units, changes in suppliers and changes in business strategies. It is important to take those factors into consideration.

You can also perform a similar analysis of budgets. In that case, the merger committee should make a comparison of the actual purchases against industry purchases. Also make a good comparison of the accounts payable that have been paid or, preferably, with expected interest rates.

Accounts Payable Ratio Analysis

Using ratio analysis is a great way to understand a company's accounts payable record. It can be a sign of profitability as well as efficiency in payments. Such analysis gives a quick view into client relations as well as how the company handles its accounts payable. By calculating the activity ratio, you will understand how effectively the target company uses its resources.

Important Accounts Payable Activity Ratios

Accounts Payable turnover = the cost of sales / Average Accounts Payable

Days Cash on Hand or Days Payable Outstanding = 365 days / Accounts Payable Turnover

It is important to understand what the meaning of accounts payable turnover is. This is the overall liquidity of a company's accounts payable. The merger committee should compare the current accounts payable turnover against the prior budget periods. If you find out that current accounts payable turnover rate is significantly lower or slower than in previous years or when compared to that of competitors, it indicates a bad credit reputation. A lower turnover level indicates that the business startup requires more cash to meet its business obligations.

XI. PRICING PLANS AND POLICIES

According to Ward (2012), the merger committee needs to review the target company business plan in order to have a good overview of the company's pricing strategy. This will allow the committee to learn how the target company sets its prices for products and/or services.

Ward (2010) continues that pricing is the most important aspect in most businesses. Many companies arrive at their pricing by calculating costs, making estimates about the benefits received by consumers, and by comparing company products with similar products and services.

XII. REVENUES AND MARGIN BY PRODUCT

The profitability of all products offered by the companies planning to merge should be evaluated by the merger committee. If some products are not generating enough income, they can be discontinued.

The merger committee should track each product margin. This analysis should be done over a period of 12 months. There are a number of software programs that can help the committee in hitting their targets. The product profit and sales ratios will play a critical role in making decisions after the merger. According to Myers (2011), knowing each product's profit margin will be useful in identifying the company's most important customers.

XIII. EXTRAORDINARY INCOME/EXPENSES

The money that a company loses or earns due to an infrequent or unusual event is called an extraordinary income or expense. When an income or expense falls into this category, the transaction must be reported and the resulting amount after tax should be separated on the income statement from the company's ordinary expenses and revenues. These extraordinary revenues and expenses are, by definition, not very common. Separating such rare transactions from the income statement helps the merger committee and other financial analysts to check on the day-to-day performance of the company without being confused by the effects of extraordinary income and expenses.

The steps listed below are used in dealing with the extraordinary income and expenses:

The company's extraordinary income should be multiplied by the income tax rate to find the tax owed if it is a profit and the tax benefits in the event of a loss. For example: assume that a business has a tax rate of 38% and suffers a $50,000 extraordinary loss caused by flood damage. The 38% is multiplied by $50,000 to get $19,000 tax savings associated with the loss.

The tax expense should be subtracted from the extraordinary income. Alternatively, you could deduct the tax savings from a loss to find the net loss. Using the example above, we subtract $19,000 from $50,000 to get $31,000 as the extraordinary net loss.

Under the extraordinary column, it should be written as extraordinary loss or extraordinary gain. This should be written below the line "Income before extraordinary items". A brief description of the extra item as well as its tax expense or benefit should be included.

The extraordinary expense or gain should be recorded together with the net taxes in the same line or in the amounts column. Any losses are enclosed in parentheses to indicate a negative value.

The extra net gain should be added to the income before the extraordinary items to find the company's net income. The resulting value is the overall profit made by the company. The extraordinary loss should be subtracted from the income before the extraordinary items to get the net income.

The net income should be reported on the last line on the income statement.

Virtually all revenues, gains, losses and expenses are reported on the income statement. There are occasionally rare events that occur during the fiscal year in addition to normal business activities. It is important that such extraordinary events be separated and recorded in a special section near the bottom of the income statement. There are two main rare items that need to be recorded separately--extraordinary items and discontinued operations. Any discontinued items are listed before any extraordinary items. Note: it is extremely unusual for a company to have both items at the same time.

Discontinued Operations

This is caused by the elimination of a large part of a company's business operations. A good example is the sale of a whole division of the company. If the eliminated division is small, then it does not qualify to be recorded as a discontinued operation.

Extraordinary Items

Extraordinary items are only those items that are unusual in nature. These are events that do not occur frequently and are outside of the company's day-to-day operations.

The merger committee should make sure no ordinary items are recorded as extraordinary. Some items, such the loss of crop due to frost or the write off of inventory due to discounting, do not qualify. These two events may be unusual, but they are not outside of the company's primary operations.

Examples of discontinued operations:

Changing Accounting Methods

This is when a company decides to change the accounting method for recording revenues and expenses. This usually happens because of changes to accounting rules set by the governing bodies. Changing such methods may require a one-time write off due to the change.

Abandoning Product lines

This happens when a company decides to stop selling some products. Often, this results in a loss because of excess, un-sold inventory. There are several reasons as to why a company can decide to abandon some products. Having to sell the products at a lower price than they paid for them is one such reason.

Restructuring and Downsizing the Business

When a company lays off personnel, they generally offer a severance package or an early retirement settlement. Such a scenario could lead to a large one-time loss.

Settling Legal Actions

Legal fees, fines and court settlements are another example of extraordinary expenses.

Writing off impaired assets

Those products that are beyond repair need to be replaced. Such damaged assets are removed from the asset accounts. It should be noted that even if assets are in good condition, if they are not able to generate income, then accounting rules require they be removed from the books.

Correcting Financial Reports for errors

If the company discovers some financial errors that were made in the past, then a catch-up correction entry is to be made. That means recording a gain or a loss that is not associated with the current year.

XIV. ANALYSIS OF MATERIAL WRITE DOWNS

Inventory write-downs contribute to many obsolescence costs. The generally accepted accounting principles (GAAP) in the U.S. show that, in most cases, inventories are recorded at cost. However, when the value of such inventories falls below the original cost, either from obsolescence or damage, the company has no option other than to write down the cost so it is consistent with the true market value. This is the best way to record the loss. The write-down is always indicated as an expense in the income statement. Any reduction in the inventory causes a loss to the company. The merger committee must make sure to factor such scenarios into their valuation of the company. Not doing so could impact the value of the merger or acquisition.

To illustrate this impact, there is a well known case of a monumental write-down at Cisco Systems, worth $2.25 billion. This event was reported to have caused a significant reduction in the company's market value. In March 2000, the company was valued at $430 billion; in March, 2001, the company was worth just S108 billion.

XV. BAD DEBT SUMMARY

Bad debts is an accounting term that refers to accounts receivable that are deemed uncollectable. The merger committee should analyze all recent and current bad debts of the target company. Appropriate measures should be taken to deal with any bad debts.

According to Day (2008), offering credit to customers generally increases sales. However, selling goods on credit creates the possibility that at least some of the payment for those goods won't be collected. Those uncollected sums should be written off accordingly. Bad debts are normally set off against sales brought about by the credit offer.

XVI. ANY OUTSTANDING CONTINGENT LIABILITIES

Contingent liabilities are defined as liabilities that are likely to occur in the future. These liabilities depend a future event and are never listed on the balance sheet, despite needing to be disclosed properly. Contingent liabilities are either implicit or explicit.

Explicit Contingent Liabilities

Explicit contingent liabilities are government business obligations specified in law or contract. The government has a duty to settle such obligations when they fall due. Examples of explicit contingent liabilities include state insurance guarantees, private investments guarantees and umbrella guarantees for a number of loans.

Implicit Contingent Liabilities

Implicit contingent liabilities are an expected burden for the government in a legal sense and are virtually always based on political pressures or even public opinion. Examples of such liabilities include:

Bank failures

Failure of the state government to pay the non-guaranteed loans

Relief and disaster financing

Failure of other funds which are not guaranteed

Outstanding contingent liabilities arise in cases like the government guaranteeing the financing of a public entity that is not creditworthy. That means that the creditors to such an entity get full recourse to the government.

XVII. ANY EXTERNAL FINANCIAL REPORTS/STUDIES

The merger committee should consider the contents of all financial studies that have been carried out on any one of the companies planning to engage in the merger. These kinds of studies can be sources of valuable information. According to GAO (2012), it is a good idea to focus on the most up-to-date information because a lot can change within a company in a short period of time.

5
TAX

a. Different jurisdictions have different tax laws, but they all view unpaid or undeclared tax with disdain. Verifying tax compliance is vital when considering a merger or acquisition

b. Items to check:

I. FEDERAL TAX RETURNS FOR THE PAST THREE YEARS

The merger committee should carefully analyze the target company's federal tax returns for at least the past three years. This is to make sure the company has no unpaid tax obligations. The newly-formed corporation will also need to report the merger to the IRS because there will inevitably be changes in tax structure after the merger. The target company's old tax return records can be obtained from the IRS by submitting IRS form 4506 for all years affected. According to TurboTax (2012), the IRS can supply copies of all federal tax returns for up to seven years.

II. LOCAL OR STATE TAX RETURNS FOR THE PAST THREE YEARS

The merger committee should strive to find out whether the two companies involved in a merger are up-to-date with all their local and state tax obligations for the past three years. In addition, the merger committee should ascertain whether the two companies planning to merge have been registered properly for state income tax withholding accounts as well as state unemployment tax. According to Russo (2011), companies should also make sure they have current information on all employees.

III. DETAILS OF ANY GOVERNMENT AUDIT

Any government audit of the two merging companies can be a great source of information. Such state or federal government reports should never be ignored. They are invaluable for getting to know the operations of the target firm.

According to GAO (2012), auditing is essential for government accountability. Government audits are preferred over private audits because they are non-partisan and objective. Such audits verify performance and ownership of a corporation. There are many different types of government audits, each with a slightly different scope. All are designed to make sure public companies are accountable for their use of public resources.

The framework for auditing is provided by the generally accepted government auditing standards (GAGAS.) These rules are used by auditors employed by government organizations.

The following are some common government audits:

Financial audits

Attestation engagements

Performance audits

IV. VAT REGISTRATION FOR EU COMPANIES

According to Privacy Solutions (2012), Value Added Tax (VAT) is a general tax in the European Union (EU) that is assessed on the value added to goods or services. Products sold in the EU are all subject to VAT. That means that all companies planning to operate in the EU must comply with VAT tax regulations.

All US-based companies wishing to export goods to the EU must process an EU VAT registration number. VAT registered sellers who sell to VAT registered buyers operating within the European Union do not need to charge VAT as long as the buyer's EU VAT registration number is stated on the sales invoice.

Businesses that are registered with VAT, but selling to buyers outside the European Union are allowed to zero-rate their supplies. The only requirement is that you provide proof that goods have been permanently exported outside the EU.

6
CONTRACTS

a. Contracts secure supplies and generate liabilities and both need to be thoroughly understood. The merger committee should also keep an eye out for any missing contracts (e.g.: no formal deal with a key supplier.)

b. Items to check:

I. BANK LENDING

Commercial banks have always competed with investment banks in lending and providing advisory services for mergers. According to Allen et al (2012), the target company generally gets a higher return when the target company's own bank certifies the value of the target company for the buyer. This doesn't happen often because buyers usually choose their own banks for such valuations.

Commercial banks also work as advisors during mergers and acquisitions. That way they end up lending money for the whole process of merger and acquisition. According to Allen et al (2012), the best commercial bank to use for a merger or acquisition is one has an existing relationship with one of the parties involved in the merger because such a bank already understands the cash flow and other financial information that isn't always accessible to outside banks. When choosing a bank as an advisor, those with prior lending relationships have a comparative advantage.

According to Chan et al (1986), information acquired by a commercial bank during a banking relationship may be re-used and even transferred to another party. This is clearly supported when we talk about underwriting activities. A bank is allowed to use the information that it has gathered over time to supply services, such as advising customers on mergers.

Allen et al (2012) further maintains that the bank's freedom to use confidential information depends on whether the merger is a friendly or hostile one. When a target company fears losing control of its business, their commercial bank may not want to use private information to advise the potential buyer. The bank, obviously, will not want to risk losing their client if the merger fails to materialize. Banks are more willing to offer advisory services when they are sure of earning large fees.

Banks that advise a target company in a merger can use the information that they have in certifying the value of the target company. You could argue that commercial banks with a prior history with the target company have a conflict of interest.

The Value of Mergers and Acquisitions

Many studies have been done to find out the value of the M&A to the target company as well as to the buyer. One such study found out that the target firms atypically have a positive return immediately after the merger announcement. On the other hand, the purchasing company usually realizes little or no immediate gain. That means that the target company gets most of the returns associated with the merger or acquisition.

II. NON-BANK LENDING

There is a lot of evidence that more and more businesses are getting loans from non-banking institutions and that such institutions are having a greater effect on mergers than ever before. According to Kang and Mullineaux (2011), nonbanks are quick to facilitate a merger because they can easily access updated information during a loan amendment process.

Nonbanks are not allowed to accept deposits. As a result, they have few regulations to deal with compared to commercial banks. According to LSTA (2007), 75 per cent of leveraged loans were offered by nonbanks in 2005.

Dennis and Mullineaux (2000) emphasizes that lenders are in a position to receive a large amount of information about their prospective borrowers during the process of approving a loan. According to LSTA (2007), all lenders are required to maintain high level of confidentiality regarding information they receive from the borrowers during the loan process. The only way they should use such information is in connection with the loan.

Several studies show that nonbanks use information they receive from clients to facilitate merger and acquisition bids. According to Ivashina et al (2008), companies that use lending banks are more likely to be targets of M&As, with their banks using the information received during the loan process.

It is common for non-banking institutions, such as insurance companies and hedge fund managers, to provide funding for M&A activities. In some cases, they even encourage firms to find new partners in the M&A market.

III. JV AGREEMENTS

Joint venture programs are permitted in many US states. In such cases, participating firms need written approval from the state's Attorney General. During a merger, the purchasing corporation must carefully scrutinize all joint ventures entered into by the target corporation to ensure that they do not violate any state laws and regulations. Such joint ventures should not threaten or affect competition in the industry. That means the joint venture should not lead to the formation of a monopoly by controlling a too large market share. Joint venture arrangements have advantages, as illustrated below:

Indivisibility

To begin with, joint ventures are largely indivisible. For example, say a technology firm wants a strong sales company so it can successfully introduce its pharmaceuticals to the world market.

Reduced Management Costs

In joint ventures, a company generally realizes fewer management costs. In such an arrangement, two or more companies maintain their own identities and working cultures, but work together towards common agreed-upon goals. According to Singh and Kogut (1998), high tech firms present a host of valuation problems. Often it is easier for the two firms to work in a joint venture arrangement.

IV. PARTNERSHIP AGREEMENTS

In United States, partnerships may be formed as unlimited liability, general partnerships or limited partnerships. There are also cases where an acquired corporation is used in a joint venture. Joint venture structures are important because they have tax advantages for both parties involved in the partnership. Foreign buyers who want to do business in real estate and natural resources are required to operate in terms of a partnership arrangement. There are extra advantages when foreign companies from Germany work in partnership with U.S. companies. These companies from Germany are exempted from taxes outside of the United States.

V. LIENS

According to Investopedia (2012), a lien is a legal right of a creditor to sell the collateral property that the debtor provided. This happens when the debtor is unable to meet his obligations as set down in a loan contract. Liens apply in cases when a person takes a loan to buy a motor vehicle. The bank that lends the money is the lien holder. That lien is usually released on completion of loan.

State laws govern liens. The only exceptions are federal tax liens. Such liens are enforced by the federal government. When a taxpayer fails to pay tax, the IRS places a legal claim against the taxpayer's property, bank accounts, vehicles or his home. In such a case, the taxpayer is not allowed to sell any of the attached property. If a taxpayer ignores the tax lien, the IRS can seize the property.

VI. EQUIPMENT LEASES

Equipment leasing is covered here in detail to make it easier for companies to understand how to treat equipment leases during a merger or acquisition. According to Block et al (2012), the Uniform Commercial Code applies to handling equipment leases as well as to general patterns of handling such transactions during a merger. Equipment leasing agreements should be evaluated by the merger committee and then either renewed or cancelled. After a decision has been made regarding each lease, transactions involving leased equipment become easier to handle. This will solve other issues, such as insurance, litigation, lease securitizations, default and remedies, and fraud. All types of leases must be checked, including merchant, cross-border, consumer, operating and leveraged leases. Some equipment is commonly leased, rather than purchased, such as computers, vessels, aircrafts and satellites.

Terms and Conditions

The merger committee needs to study the terms and conditions of each lease so that they understand how to transfer or terminate these leases.

VII. MORTGAGES AND OTHER LOANS

Loans and mortgages that exist at the time of merger should be closely accessed by the merger committee so they know to transfer them to the new company.

VIII. INSURANCE CONTRACTS

The merger committee should thoroughly review insurance contracts held by both the buyer and the seller as early as possible. Sometimes, additional costs come to light after the sale has been concluded. If these new costs are not adequately covered by insurance, the merger can turn into a disaster.

According to King & Spalding (2012), many insurance issues should be dealt with during the due diligence stage. To avoid acquiring liabilities that are not well covered by insurance, the committee should audit the target company's insurance coverage. The following steps should be followed in checking insurance issues:

The merger committee should determine the uninsured liabilities and carefully review all the insurance policies and claims.

All the seller's prior and current insurance policies should be evaluated to make sure that all main risks are well covered.

Key contracts should be reviewed to learn about any transfer provisions. They may have placed additional insured status on customers, corporate affiliates and suppliers. Not dealing with this issue could put the seller's assets at risk. In addition, key contracts should be reviewed to expose any insurance that may be available to the seller from other parties.

When a company is acquiring operations in an unfamiliar location, the merger committee should look to identify any new exposures. Find out whether it is possible to purchase the new coverage or whether the commercial property schedules should be up-dated to make sure that the operations are covered in the event of a catastrophe.

According to Airmic (2012), each and every merger and acquisition deal is different. However, there are some common practices that can be used in most cases to reduce any uncertainty. Insurance can be used to lessen any surprises during the post-merger period. In case of a hostile bid, the transaction is very different. Very little sharing of information occurs and the merger committee has to rely, for the most part, on the information available in the public domain, such as audited accounts.

IX. SUPPLIER CONTRACTS

A merger can create a lot of uncertainty among target company suppliers, and some companies will decide to terminate their supplier contracts. Usually, supplier contracts do not have an exit clause in the event of a merger.

X. VENDOR CONTRACTS

According to Moore (2012), many financial institutions have what are called vendor contracts. Such businesses offer contracts to other firms to provide software systems that touch on electronic banking, operational systems and even document platforms. Even small firms can spend thousands of dollars for such services via vendor contracts.

The merger committee should take its time in evaluating these vendor contracts to learn whether their services will be needed after the merger. Remember to also scrutinize the wording in vendor contracts. Moore (2012) maintains that often the terms and wording in such contracts is different from what has been discussed.

Emphasis should be placed on vendor accountability as well as retaining a high level of flexibility after the merger process. When the merger committee decides to end a vendor contract, it's a good idea to ask for recommendations on new vendors from businesses that have received services from your prospective vendors. Usually, it's unwise to be the first client for a new vendor. It also makes sense to be cautious when dealing with a vendor whose management structure has changed. Start by identifying your company's needs before looking for a vendor.

According to Los Angeles (2005), vendor contracts should be evaluated by the merger committee at the bidding or proposal stage. This is because after a notification is made about a pending merger, the Secretary of State's office will carry out a careful review of the impact of the merger on vendor contracts.

Transition to a new vendor

Before signing vendor contract services, make sure that the services that they offer are compatible with your company needs. Be very specific when quantifying services and which vendors you want to provide those services. It's not out of line to ask a vendor to provide some testing services to see if they are a good fit for your company. Vendors should have deadlines, and there should be penalties for failing to meet such deadlines.

The merger committee should make arrangements for a back-up plan so that there is no panic if new vendor services fail to work as expected or are not ready within the proposed time frame.

Any contract that the merger committee signs with the vendors should include all terms of the contract, such as how frequently the vendor should provide maintenance services and the minimum number of services that the vendor must provide annually.

XI. OTHER CONTRACTS

Many contracts are directly affected in a merger or acquisition. According to Moore (2012), the terms and conditions of all other contracts should be read carefully to see if they include a provision about a merger or acquisition.

The new company will also need to transfer Internet protocol (IP) numbers, also referred to as autonomous system numbers (ASNs.) Mergers and acquisitions usually prompt the need for a transfer of IP numbers.

There are several steps involved in changing IP addresses:

Requirements

IP registration is issued by ARIN and not transferable to other parties. Therefore, you'll need to seek written permission from ARIN to make such a transfer. This organization is set up to facilitate such transfers.

Request Submission

The company formed after a merger should establish point of contact (POC) handles as well as the organization identifier with ARIN. The company will need to complete a transfer request form that should be accompanied by the API key to aid in processing the request.

According to ARIN, the transfer of IP due to a merger or acquisition should be submitted by the company's Website administrator or POC and needs to have documentation attached that supports the merger, such as a final court order.

7
OFFICIAL

a. Many areas require various business licenses. These will need to be transferred to the new owner.

b. Items to check:

I. COPIES OF PERMITS

Companies in the United States have a number of business licenses and permits, depending on what type of business they operate. According to Cornell University (2007), these include general business permits, certificates of occupancy, building permits, permits to operate certain equipment and machinery, boiler permits and vehicle registration and licenses. Some businesses, such as franchises, also need special licenses. Most of these permits can be transferred easily after a merger or acquisition, but in some cases, the new company will have to apply for new licenses. The buyer should make arrangements to transfer permits so that they will be ready to use after the deal closes.

In most cases, government permits are not assignable after a merger or acquisition. The buyer is therefore urged to find out if it is possible to get new permits before the deal closes.

II. COPIES OF LICENSES

According to Cornell University (2007), a buyer will need to check with the appropriate authorities and/or agencies to make sure that their licenses will be honored after a merger or acquisition. Some U.S. states, including Connecticut and New Jersey, require that licenses be approved by the appropriate authorities before the acquisition process is completed.

III. REGISTRATION CERTIFICATES

Registration certificates will need to be adjusted to reflect the merger or conversion. For example, the Texas Secretary of State (2013) requires filing form 415 to make changes to company registration certificates.

IV. REPORTS TO OFFICIAL BODIES

The target company may have drafted reports that were later submitted to official bodies. These reports should be scrutinized to determine that the information submitted is consistent with company records.

V. REQUEST FROM OFFICIAL BODIES

All paperwork having to do with information requests to official bodies should be studied carefully during the due diligence process.

8
LITIGATION

a. Litigation, even when you are in the right, can be extremely expensive, so an understanding of any on-going or potential lawsuits is vital. The absence of litigation should be a seller warranty.

b. Items to check:

I. PENDING LITIGATION AGAINST THE TARGET COMPANY

Many lawsuits arise from a failure to comply with law. It should be understood from the outset that in the United States, the buyer in a merger inherits the legal responsibilities associated with property purchased during a merger or acquisition. Environmental non-compliance issues, for example, have the potential to cause severe problems for the buyers if full disclosures is not made during due diligence. The seller should disclose any failure to comply with environmental laws. If there are any harmful waste materials in any of the real property acquired, that must be reported upfront so the buyer can factor that into the valuation of the company. Remember that it is very expensive to remove hazardous waste materials. It calls for a phase I environmental audit of the premises. After that audit, there may be a need for a phase II and even a phase III audit if any issues are found. Such audits include water, soil and air tests and are instrumental in determining the presence or the extent of any environmental problems. Note that it is the duty of the buyer to find out whether any hazardous waste disposal was done in the past and whether it was done in accordance with state, local and federal laws. This is necessary because a buyer can be held liable for any improper waste disposal outside of company premises.

Make sure as a buyer you find out whether there are any pending litigations regarding non-compliance with the law. According to Krishnan et al (2011), there are a number of cases in which the stockholders sue directors of the target company with the allegations that those directors have violated their fiduciary duty by selling their company for too low a price.

II. POTENTIAL LIABILITY

There are many possible sources of liability. Non-compliance with local, state and federal law can lead to huge fines on your company. As a buyer, you must also make sure that the target company is compliant with zoning laws. This is important because insurance does not cover compliance with zoning laws. The target company must also be compliant with health and occupational safety laws. The seller should disclose if their company has received any notices for non-compliance to any laws. Litigation is expensive, particularly cases that deal with equal opportunity and hiring practices. A buyer can request the seller to be responsible for any pre-closing non-compliance.

III. POTENTIAL COSTS

Several things can incur potential costs such as the marketing of the merger. According to Anderson (2012), it is a good idea to market the merger well because the merger committee has a duty to affect the way the merger is viewed by the industry, clients and prospective clients. The best approach to marketing is to have all the executives and staff say the same thing about the merger. They should explain how they see great things in the future as a result of the merger. Additional costs will include hiring a public relations consultant to prepare press releases on the merger. These activities can be carried out before, during and after the merger. When marketing is done well, it can have a powerful impact on the merger. On the other hand, poor public relations can have competitors claiming that it is just a merger of a couple of bad firms.

Anderson (2012) maintains that the new company should prepare information about the merger to send to others in the industry as well as clients and even prospective clients. Always highlight the new strengths that will be realized by the merger. A good example is the diversification and specialization brought as a result of a merger.

Some feel that holding small client receptions so that the clients can be familiar with the new management faces is beneficial.

IV. PENDING LITIGATION BY THE TARGET COMPANY

Some lawsuits are filed by the target company against other companies, individuals and even the government. According to Krishnan (2011), a target company can sue a prospective bidder for violating state or federal corporate laws. There might also be some pending litigation regarding violation of antitrust laws.

V. POTENTIAL LIABILITY

There are many sources of potential liability that must be factored in during the pre-acquisition stage. You must check whether there are any union agreements. If there are, read the union contracts to determine the best compensation and benefits strategy. Then determine how that affects the committee's liability assessment.

By reviewing the company records, you will quickly get a feel for whether the target company's way of conducting business is organized or unorganized. This will likely be apparent as you review documents during the due diligence process. A haphazard approach to records and management could likely mean trouble later on.

The committee must take enough time to gain an in-depth review of the target company during the due diligence phase. This is important to avoid being surprised later on by liabilities that were never anticipated.

VI. POTENTIAL COSTS

According to the U.S. Trade Commission (1997), mergers generally cause a company to operate more efficiently due to a reduction in costs. Jeziorski (2011) agrees that potential costs, such as administrative and operations costs are reduced when two firms merge, and the combined company often becomes more effective by producing products at a lower cost.

VII. SETTLEMENT DOCUMENTATION

There are basically two methods used for closing a public merger transaction. To begin the merger process, a definitive agreement has to be reached between the buyer and the seller. There is a one-step and a two-step merger offer.

The two-step tender offer is the quickest method of closing merger deals. Using this method, the tender offer stage lasts for a minimum of 20 days. If more than 90 percent of the target company's shareholders vote in favor of the merger, the result is a short form merger. When this 90 percent threshold cannot be reached, proxy statements have to be mailed to the shareholders for a formal vote.

The one-step proxy statement path generally takes around 8-10 weeks to get the shareholder vote. This is the most widely used method. In this stage, a majority of votes is required. In some cases, the corporate charter and state law may require a super majority.

VIII. EMPLOYEE LITIGATION AND CLAIMS

You must identify all the on-going disputes with current and former employees or any employee situations that are likely to develop into a lawsuit. The committee must try to set a potential risk value on these lawsuits.

IX. PATENT ACTIONS

It is quite surprising that the courts and other agencies responsible have never come up with an antitrust framework to be used in solving patent disputes between companies. According to Creighton and Sher (2009), it is a common practice for firms having such disputes to settle them out of court. Pharmaceutical cases are unusual in that any infringement is rarely disputed. A merger can be used to solve such patent disputes.

X. INTELLECTUAL PROPERTY ACTIONS

All actions regarding intellectual property should be examined by the merger committee to find out whether there is a way to settle them out of court and so that the committee can evaluate any future consequences of such actions.

9
PRODUCTS

a. What the target company sells (products or services) must be fully understood for a successful merger.

b. Items to check:

I. PRODUCT AND SERVICE OFFERING

This is the product mix that a company offers to its customers. Some companies have a wide product offering, while others concentrate on just a few products or services.

II. MARKET SHARE BY PRODUCT

A company's performance in the market can rarely be measured simply by sales figures. To get a clear picture, you should also evaluate changes in sales and market share.

To measure a company's performance in relation to that of its competitors, you need to measure the portion of the market that the firm is able to reach with its products and services.

The market proportion is reflected as follows:

Market Share = Total Sales made by a firm/ Total Market Sales

Sales Value = sales price x sales volume

Some businesses define sales as the number of units that are shipped or, preferably, the number of customers that use the company's products or services.

The merger committee will have easy access to sales figures because these records are always kept by the target company. Finding the total market sales figures is more difficult. Such information can be found from trade associations and by doing a little market research.

Reasons to Increase Market Share

The larger the markets share, the higher the profitability. Below are some of the reasons why a surviving firm could prefer to increase its market share.

Companies with a greater market share often have a better reputation

There are economies of scale when a company sells more products.

A company with a larger market share has increased bargaining power with suppliers.

How to Increase Market Share

There are three primary ways to increase market share:

The market share can be increased by changing pricing, by offering promotions and by producing high quality products.

The company can adopt an intensive distribution network.

The following are some additional ways a company can change its marketing mix:

Promotion

Advertising expense can be increased in order to capture a wider market share. This can be effective if competitors do not respond with equal measures.

Product

Features or components of products can be upgraded to offer superior value to the customers.

Distribution

The distribution frequency should be increased in addition to adding new distribution channels.

Price

When the price of a company's products is volatile, any decrease in price will lead to increased sales revenue.

III. TOTAL MARKET SIZE(S)

The merger committee should find out the total market size for the industry in which the surviving organization does business in order to plan intelligently.

IV. INVENTORY ANALYSIS

Inventory analysis is a method used in to find the highest level of company inventory. There are two formulas for carrying calculating this:

Number of days in inventory = inventory at the end of accounting period/average cost of goods on daily basis.

Inventory turnover = cost of goods sold/average inventory

V. INVENTORY VALUATION

Inventory valuation is used to ascertain the inventory turnover and determine how often the company buys raw materials or items to resell during the year.

The following is the formula used to find inventory valuation:

Inventory Turnover = Cost of Goods Sold/ (Starting Inventory + Ending Inventory) /2)

Example:

Warehouse Inventory Turnover = $50,000M/ ((12,000M + $13,000)/2) = 4.22

VI. OBSOLESCENCE POLICY

Most companies strive to produce the best products for their consumers. They have, therefore, invested a lot of their time in offering high value products. Product obsolescence is the final stage of the product life cycle, the sixth stage in that cycle.

Many companies have an obsolescence policy that outlines ways of dealing with products that have become obsolete. There are many reasons why products become obsolete. These include such things as the introduction of new goods and technologies to the market place (technical obsolescence), products that no longer meet government standards (components obsolescence), or obsolescence due to the lower market demand (economic obsolescence.)

VII. PRODUCT BACKLOG ANALYSIS

The following techniques are used in backlog analysis:

Kano analysis

Kano analysis is used in classifying product features in different categories. It covers basic attributes and identifies which products are important to satisfying users.

Theme-screening

Theme-screening uses baseline themes as well as customer reports.

Theme scoring

There are many benefits to monitoring the product backlog closely.

VIII. PRODUCT SEASONALITY

Seasonality refers to fluctuations in sales and output at different times of the year. Many products have such variations. Note that short term fluctuations experienced over one week or day do not have the same impact on the company as seasonal changes in sales patterns.

Demand or supply?

It is important to identify the difference between seasonality of demand and seasonality of supply.

There are certain products whose production depends on weather and seasonal changes. For some industries, such as agriculture and horticulture, seasonality in supply is an important factor, although even in these industries there are instances when seasonality does not come into play, such as when greenhouses are used. On the other hand, manufactured products are not usually affected by weather or seasonal changes.

Seasonal demand

Seasonal factors do not usually impact production and supply of manufactured goods, however, their demand can and often does depend on seasonal fluctuations, at least to some extent. For example, some products have a high seasonal demand, such as swimwear, Christmas cards, fireworks and sun block.

IX. MAJOR SUPPLIERS

The merger committee should identify the target company's primary suppliers at the onset of their analysis. These are the people who help the business to succeed by providing the necessary materials. The goal of the committee should be to retain such suppliers even after the merger or acquisition since it is often difficult to find reliable suppliers.

X. SUPPLIER SPEND ANALYSIS

Spend analysis (SAS) sheds additional light on information pertaining to procurement, making it possible for the committee to track how much is spent on suppliers, commodities, services and products. SAS is a good tool for reducing costs, maintaining purchasing power, and improving supplier relationships.

Benefits

Benefits of SAS include reducing the amount of money the company spends for inventory and raw materials. By ranking suppliers as preferred and non-preferred, it also helps to build better vendor relations.

Features

Some SAS features include ranking of suppliers, a high quality of data, a high visibility of procurement data and reporting.

Supply Spend Analysis

Transforming data into opportunity

This is a unique process that involves talking about making improvements to supply chain management by analyzing carefully on what, how and to whom the company spends money.

Supply opportunities

There are several processes involved with collecting and analyzing data relating to your company's spending, validating the spending against the general ledger to get the level of accuracy, matching the main supplier file against the D & B database to get insight into the suppliers and their interrelationships, and identifying potential opportunities to minimize spending.

Supplier relationships

There are several ways to analyze supplier relationships. These include identifying any duplicate suppliers, finding out the relationship between various suppliers to improve your relations when signing contracts, discovering if a particular supplier has any risks associated with it, and checking to see if the supplier's identification out of line with acceptable D & B accuracy.

This analysis will help you to tell if your supplier will be able to meet all your purchase needs, helping you to deliver a good product at a competitive price. Most supply management chains have two modules--supply intelligence and supply base optimization. The former enables you to identify the right suppliers by focusing on your sourcing goals, while the later automates your system to work with only the current supplier information.

10
MARKETING

a. Every business should know and understand its competitors and its key clients; verify that the target company understands and has delivered this basic need.

b. Items to check:

I. COMPETITORS

All the company's competitors should be identified as part of the vesting process.

II. COMPETITORS MARKET SHARE

The merger committee should find what percentage of the market belongs to the target company's competitors. This is important for setting strategies to take away some of that market share.

III. MAJOR CLIENTS

The merger committee should also identify the target company's major clients, those who order large quantities of goods and services. Everything possible should be done to retain such customers.

IV. MAJOR CLIENT INCOME

The merger committee should also evaluate how much income those major clients bring to the target company and whether those clients are in a position to buy more from the surviving company.

V. PRICING STRATEGY

Pricing is one of the four major elements in any marketing mix. Setting prices for products or services cannot be overlooked because it helps determine not only sales, but other marketing elements, such as channel decisions, promotions and product features.

There is no single rule that can be used to determine pricing. However, you can use the following steps to get a good idea of what price you should set:

Develop marketing strategy- You need to perform marketing analysis, targeting, segmentation, and positioning.

Making marketing decisions- These include what product definition, distribution and promotional tactics to use.

Estimate the demand curve- Learn how sales vary with price

Calculate cost- Include all the costs incurred in making and distributing the product.

Seek to understand environmental factors- Evaluate how competitors set pricing and understand legal constraints, for example.

Set pricing goals - These can include maximizing revenue, stabilizing prices or maximizing profits.

Determine pricing- Using information collected in all the steps outlined above, you can now select an appropriate pricing method to guide you in developing a pricing structure and defining discounts.

The above steps are intended as guidelines. These steps are interrelated and do not have to be performed in the order given. Pricing goals often depend on a number of factors, such as production cost, economies of scale, product differentiation, company resources and the expected elasticity of demand of the product.

Competitor-based pricing

When competition is strong, customers have more choices and multiple sources for a particular product. They may choose the supplier with the highest quality product or the cheapest provider.

In an perfect world, no company would have enough market influence to be able to set prices above their competitors. Most companies tend to set prices that are in line with the prices charged by direct competitors. Such companies become price takers since they must accept the going market price as determined by the forces of demand and supply.

Using competitor pricing has an advantage because selling prices are in line with those of rivals, so price is not a competitive disadvantage. The problem becomes how to determine non-price ways of competing, such as offering better availability and/or providing memorable customer service.

Pricing methods:

Managers may use several pricing methods to arrive at the final product price. These methods include:

Cost pricing --Setting prices at production cost plus a certain profit margin

Targeting return pricing -- Setting prices to achieve a target return-on-investment

Value based pricing -- Giving a quote that is attractive to customers relative to prices of other products already on the market

Psychological pricing -- Basing the price on factors, such as product quality and what consumers perceive to be fair pricing

VI. MARKETING COLLATERAL

Marketing collateral is a collection of marketing communications used as part of the company's overall marketing strategy. Many things can be considered marketing collateral, including data sheets and brochures about company products and white papers of a technical nature.

VII. BROCHURES ETC.

Having effective brochures is a proven and effective way of spreading the word about company products, services and activities. Other effective marketing tools include posters, catalogs, business cards and postcards, among others. It can be very challenging to produce high quality materials for promotion purposes, especially in designing and printing them. The merger committee should work in collaboration with printers, writers and designers to come up with the best brochures possible for the surviving company.

VIII. SALES PROJECTIONS BY PRODUCT

Product sales projections can be challenging for any business owner. The merger committee should work to evaluate existing sales projections by brand. It is much easier to project sales for existing companies than for start-ups where there is no historical data.

To forecast sales for a new service or product, you must start by breaking sales into smaller units. Projections should be done for every unit sales. The number of projected units is multiplied by price to calculate sales volume.

IX. COMMISSION STRUCTURE

11
PERSONNEL

a. Employees are usually a company's most valuable resource, and it is important to do everything possible to remain existing employees after the merger.

b. Items to check:

I. ORGANIZATIONAL CHART

Per AON (2012): every time two companies combine via a merger or acquisitions, the organizations chart for the two companies changes. This change is necessary to achieve new goals, but the success of the new combined company depends on how well all of the parties involved in the merger are able to switch from two entities to one company. Organizational change demands that you prepare your team well by creating a compelling vision statement and working to overcome any resistance to change by explaining why this change will be good for the company and for them. You will be need to senior management to create this new organizational mission and define new goals and objectives for the new, combined company.

Two merging companies can play different roles. In some cases, the target company takes over branding once the deal is completed. There are many types of mergers. Competing companies may merge to form a new entity. In a vertical merger, a company merges with one of its customers. Whatever the case, the merger should reflect a new identity, even in its organizational structure. Care must be taken when you are forced to remove redundancy in the new company.

When working on the organizational chart, it's a good idea to involve your employees on all stages of decision making, if possible, and allow them to ask questions. Study the corporate culture of the two companies. You will need to plan carefully if you have two companies that have been run with opposite management styles. To merge the two cultures, you'll need to identify the best of both organizations.

According to AON (2012), the best way to introduce changes is by charging your employees with initiating the changes. The new organization's vision should be perceived as addressing current problems and leading to a more agreeable work environment. All company activities and programs must be aligned with the new strategic plan.

You will need to be patient and allocate enough time for the transition to take place. Employees will need to be prepared to let go of their old habits and adopt new ones. It normally takes time to get used to working with new people in new places. The new company should put in place a coaching program that helps employees understand their new roles. This should be followed by an orientation program.

Using your indicators, you should monitor the company's operations. You can start by evaluating customer satisfaction over a period of six months. Adjustments should be made so the new company is received positively by customers.

You can communicate the changes even more using Web sites, email and online newsletters. It is also a good idea to make use of the social media, blogs and forums. Here you can give a detailed explanation of the changes that will take place because of the merger. With good communication, you can usually avoid the spread of rumors and propaganda. Any employee retention strategy must start early, before the merger and acquisition starts. Retaining key talent is important to any successful company.

Many companies use retention agreements with their employees. Those companies that have been involved in mergers and acquisitions before usually have a higher employee retention rate. Some companies retain all employees or at least a majority of the acquired company's employees. In North America, it's not uncommon for employers to offer retention bonuses.

You can also use performance-based incentives as retention bonuses.

Employees from both the purchasing and the target company will naturally be concerned about their job future. Because of this, the merger committee should not only focus on administrative issues, but the human ones as well. Employees realize that some adjustments will need to be made to combine the two companies. Those employees whose job descriptions overlap may find themselves out of a job. Usually, combining the companies only affects a small portion of the workforce. However, the truth is that virtually all employees will be worried. To help ease employees' doubts, you must keep them informed. When it comes time to combine a few departments, let employees know ahead of time, giving them as much information as possible. Poor communications will only increase doubt and dissension among your employees. They value their job security as much as you value your company.

II. BLOGS FOR SENIOR STAFF

Mergers are never complete until they are formally closed. The two companies need, therefore, to prepare proper communication plans for announcing the merger after closing. According to Harrison (2013), your M&A communications should largely focus on senior staff, customers, key suppliers, shareholders and other partner companies.

Start by appointing a couple of spokespeople for each audience as well as a preferred communications channel. Next, create an activity calendar, starting right from the day of announcement through the 90 day period leading to the proposed closing date.

Communication from the senior staff can come from various departments. The purchasing company should learn to use the most influential individual from all departments to facilitate internal communication. According to Davenport and Barrow (2012), senior staff members in corporate communications and public relations departments will be at the key players in communicating the merger. The director of corporate communication will play a vital role in convincing shareholders and media to support the merger or acquisition. This will involve a lot of work. Some communications overlap. There are employees who own stock in the company and shareholders who read the newspaper. Customers also share information with employees. You'll need to devise a separate communication plan for each group of people. The important thing is to be consistent with the message across all communications plans.

Role played by Senior Staff in Human Resources

Senior human resources staff need to contribute their expertise in handling people with different education and attitudes. These are also the people with the best knowledge and understanding of the union representatives and of the corporate culture as a whole. These employees will play a key role in selling the merger to the rest of the employees. The HR department is also in the best position to answer employee benefit questions.

Senior Staff at the Marketing Department

Senior marketing executives are the people closest to customers. They understand the company brands and products and they can assure customers that they will continue to meet their needs. The marketing department will help to create a solid foundation for creating the company brand after the merger or acquisition process is completed.

Senior Staff in the CEO's office

The senior employees in the CEO's office have at their disposal the most up-to-date information on the merger or acquisition. These staff members can get a lot accomplished just by using the CEO's name and have most likely developed strong relationships and alliances with employees in other departments.

Communication experts play an important role in helping leaders streamline their message to various stakeholders. These experts should be involved as early as possible to help senior staff members streamline and solidify their message. All communications from the purchasing company should build a great story on why the merger or acquisition is necessary and desirable.

It is very important that leaders from both the acquiring and the target companies match their actions with their words. These leaders will be under constant scrutiny from employees, so they need to be true to their words.

Devenport and Barrow (2012) further maintain that communication experts should not invent a good story that will be undermined by the actions and words of the company leaders. In such cases, it is wiser to have a consistent story despite the fact that it may be less attractive to the audience.

Staff Communication is essential

There is very little that the company can say about integration until the deal closes officially. Instead of keeping silent, you should actually increase the rate of communication. There are some small and large issues that you can tackle without divulging too much. According to Harrison (2013), the finance and accounting departments will have plenty to keep them busy during this time. It is important to use internal activity to provide small amounts of information that will reassure employees of all ranks. This kind of communication will help lessen the tension caused by the announcement of the proposed merger.

Communication should be done relentlessly

Tensions commonly escalate on both sides during a merger or acquisition. This happens with employees and the management. Fears arise because it is obvious that cost savings require removing any redundancies. The employees in duplicate positions fear losing their jobs. So do those employees who make the smallest contribution to the organization. Organizational changes are inevitable during a merger. The only variable is the size and breath of those changes.

Both companies should be in constant communication with their employees during the period before the merger or acquisition closes. Where there is little communication, there will generally be increased uneasiness among the workers and low morale.

After making the final touches on the deal, the company should use their respective senior management teams to ensure that the new company works well. After the deal closes, the first challenge is to mesh the communication style of the two companies. As you wait to integrate the two companies, senior managers need to work as a team in explaining the new decision making processes.

Stage	Communication to Audience	Content
Pre-merger or acquisition	Realities in the industry	Address rumors and current fears.
Due-diligence	None	None
Announcement	Quick communication to media heads. Ensure consistency in the main points.	Address current rumors and fears Address reactions to announcements Evaluate current knowledge of the workforce on the merger or acquisition
Stage between announcement and completion	Process and timetable Start making announcements on strategy and structure	Address current rumors and fears Listen to views from representatives about the proposed merger or acquisition
Day One	Consistent main messages Initial reasons and decisions	Channels for individual views Address fears and rumors

III. LABOR/EMPLOYMENT DISPUTES

The purchasing company is charged with learning whether there are any current labor union issues, such as slowdowns, strikes and lock-outs.

IV. EMPLOYEE COMPENSATION PLANS

According to Financial Directions (2009), issues related to employee compensation plans are the most complex to deal with during pre- as well as post-acquisition phases. The merger committee must therefore put aside sufficient time to work on these compensation plans. Ideally, this process should take place during the pre-acquisition phase. During the post-acquisition period, there will be little time to work on those plans satisfactorily since there will be so much else to accomplish. Dealing with employee compensation issues early is key to a smooth transition.

V. PENSION PLANS

Retirement plans should be part of the benefit review process and should be discussed with stakeholders. Explain in detail how the new firm will exchange years of service from the old pension plan to the new one. Often, the new company brings in employees from the acquired firm on the sale date. Usually, such employees are not subject to any new hire waiting period.

VI. OPTION/PROFIT SHARE PLANS

Options and profit share plans are a good way to promote financial security for employees upon retirement and such plans benefit both employees and employers.

Why employers start profit sharing plans?

A well-established profit sharing plan can help attract and keep valuable employees.

The employers can choose when and how much to contribute to the profit sharing plan.

Such plans are very flexible.

Money contributed can be invested in stocks, mutual, mutual funds, and other financial investment options.

Contributions to many plans are not taxed by the state or federal government until the money is taken out of the plan.

Employees are allowed to take their contributions with them if they leave the company, easing administrative processing.

Establishing a Profit Sharing Plan

A company can either establish a profit sharing plan itself or hire the services of a financial institution, such as a bank, insurance company or mutual fund provider. These institutions will guide you through the process of establishing and maintaining the profit sharing plan. There are four basic steps involved in setting up a profit sharing plan:

Adopt an existing written plan document; this document serves a guide and foundation for day-to-day operations. This document will likely be provided by the person you hire to guide you through the process of setting up the plan. If not, then you will need to get one from a financial institution or a retirement plan professional. In either case, you will be bound by bound by the terms of the plan document.

Arrange a trust fund for the plan's assets, all assets to be owned by the plan must be held in trust to ensure they are used solely to benefit the participants and their beneficiaries. At least one trustee should be charged with handling contributions, investments and distributions. Selecting a trustee should be done with care because the financial integrity of the plan depends on the trustee. However, if you have no one to trust or that has time to administer the plan, you can set up the plan as a contract with an insurance company.

In such a case, you will not need to have a trustee since the contracts are held by the insurance company, not in trust.

VII. MANAGEMENT INCENTIVES

Some different management incentives are listed as follows:

a. Stock options

b. Stock ownership

c. Long-term incentive plans

d. Equity based compensation among others

When boards use the stock-based compensation as an incentive during mergers, they can often achieve higher performance levels as well as prevent management from leaving the company.

According to Line and Amland (2011), CEOs are more risk averse than most shareholders. This explains why they are usually compensated well in the merger contract. It has been noted that when a firm faces annual standard deviations of billions of dollars, such contracts cost shareholders an appreciable amount of money.

Using long-term incentive plans is also a great way of incentifying management. Such plans are set by the board of directors in contract with the CEO. For example, say the board of directors fixes accounting performance goals for a period of three or five years. The incentive is set so that the CEO will be rewarded if those goals are met. Another type of long-term incentive plan is stock-based bonuses.

VIII. OPTIONS/PROFIT SHARE

A merger will be more useful when the surviving company is in a better position to compete than the two firms that formed the merger were separately. This new, stronger company should also generate more sales opportunities, a better market position and thus more money for profit share plans.

IX. NON-CASH PAYMENTS

There are several payments that can be made to the employees to even out any inequities caused by the merger. This compensation is designed to attract employees of the target company to work for the new company after the merger.

According to Frederiksen and Sinkin (2012), several things can be done to retain employees after a merger. Below are just a few non-cash incentives that can help retain employees:

Free or discounted parking

Employment entertainment allowances

Travel allowances

Discounted meals at a company cafeteria or lunch room

X. NON-SALARY COMPENSATION

According to Frederiksen and Sinkin (2012), during a merger, the buyer should attempt to retain as many employees as possible. Not doing so can easily result in a failed merger. They further maintain that perquisites may not be the most important factors in employee compensation. The buyer will lose employees if the employees feel they are being under-paid. That's how non-salary compensation, such as vacation time, paid health insurance and sick days, can help.

XI. MEDICAL AND OTHER INSURANCE

According to Frederiksen and Sinkin (2012), covering 100 percent of medical insurance is a sure way to retain employ-ees and prevent looming disaster that can arise if a majority of the target company employees leave the new company. In addition, the merger committee must check on any on-going and expensive medical claims. These must be considered as liabilities as you set the target company valuation.

XII. CARS, TRAVEL ETC.

During a merger, there are employees with cars provided by the company to use for travel and company business. Frederiksen and Sinkin (2012) maintain that during a merg-er, more senior employees should be allocated cars for busi-ness travel as a way of encouraging them to stay with the company after the merger.

XIII. EMPLOYEE AGREEMENTS

Employee agreements need be evaluated during the merg-er process to learn if they have enforceable and/or clearly assignable clauses. If it is possible to amend or replace any employee agreement, this needs to be done before the merger.

The buyer should look to see if there are any unwanted employee contracts that need to be canceled. It is also the buyer's responsibility to evaluate all bargaining agreements during the due diligence process. Thought needs to be given on how to deal with competition from employees who may decide to resign due to the merger or acquisition. Try to ensure business continuity up to the closing. In some cases, pre-merger agreements may be necessary.

XIV. CONFIDENTIALITY

According to Batterson (2012), it is common for participating corporations to keep information about the merger private by having all parties sign confidentiality agreements at the beginning of the merger or acquisition process. This agreement must be respected and is legally binding. Confidentiality agreements are useful for many reasons. They put restrictions on how much information can be disclosed, and they prohibit using information obtained during the merger process for any other purpose.

The confidentiality agreement usually holds the buyer responsible for any breach of confidentiality by the buyer's agents and/or employees. Such agents and employees have to be told about the nature of the confidentiality agreement. The agreement outlines who should have access to confidential information obtained from the target company. Such an agreement can even block some persons from accessing the information or portions of that information. Examples of this sensitive information include sources of equity financing and debt. Such agreements need to have time restrictions. In most cases, the potential buyers will request a period of 12 to 24 months. Target companies usually request a period of between two and five years. The length of this time period depends on the sensitivity of the information disclosed. Most such agreements are valid for 18 to 24 months.

A confidentiality agreement will give you access to key target company employees. Such an agreement has clauses that prevent the buyer from hiring employees who work for the target corporation (before the merger is completed.) The target corporation is allowed to carry out some due diligence of its own on the prospective buyers. The seller will look for issues like whether the buyer's securities are being used as collateral for the deal.

It is important to keep matters strictly confidential before announcing the merger or the acquisition. It will be a big mistake if shareholders, customers, employees and suppliers are allowed to find out about the intended merger before the deal is ready to be announced. This can also have a damaging effect on the target company. That company will likely lose value and key employees as a result of the leak and customers may switch to the competing corporations. Such leaked information may also hurt productivity and cause suppliers not to renew their contracts with the target company. Therefore, it is important to have the two participating companies sign a confidentiality agreement.

A confidentiality agreement usually prohibits the acquiring corporation from contacting the employees, owners, owners and other people associated with the company to be acquired.

The company should also make sure that they do not distribute any information regarding the company to outside parties. They should also agree to never to use the information they get for purposes other than the proposed merger evaluation.

XV. NON-COMPETE

Non-compete agreements are signed between employers and employees to prevent employees from leaving the company and competing with their former employer. According to Marx et al (2012), a 2010 Georgia non-compete law places restrictions on the type of jobs that a former employee can enter for a period of one to two years after leaving a company. Employees can also be required to sign non-disclosure agreements. Such agreements are meant to protect trade secrets.

Non-compete laws were changed by four states in 2008. Some of these states expanded on the right to use the law, while other states restricted the enforceability of the law. The State of New York and the State of Oregon placed additional restrictions on companies using non-compete agreements. On the other hand, the State of Louisiana and the State of Idaho expanded the power of non-compete laws in their states. US federal law does not address non-compete agreements.

XVI. IPR PROTECTION

The two companies involved in a merger or acquisition must work on matters of IPR by protecting their respective intellectual property and other confidential information.

XVII. CONSULTANTS

The number of mergers and acquisitions has recently increased. Consultants are good experts to for making mergers or acquisitions easier. Most business professionals participate in few mergers during their careers. Consultants, on the other hand, are involved in numerous merger transactions each year. Why not make use of this experience? Below are seven areas where mergers and acquisitions consultants can help:

Pro Forma Budget

Consultants can work as a third party to review the financial records of the target company to arrive at a pro forma budget for the resulting firm. Consultants should be hired to help in ensuring that the figures are workable for the new corporation. The idea of creating the pro forma makes it possible for consultants to review all aspects of the firms in their former identities as well as how they will operate after the merger. They are in a good position to expose any potential problems and to make sound recommendations on how to handle any problems.

Handling Agreements

It is a good idea to form a merger agreement as soon as possible to prevent any information about the merger from leaking. A consultant can help set up the proper terms for such agreement and can be required to set the guidelines for the work leading up to the merger or acquisition process.

Interviews

The interviews conducted by a third party, such as a consultant, are usually more successful than those conducted by a vested party. Partners are less likely to view such interviews as malicious. People will also be more likely to express any fears and concerns to the consultant than to someone who works for either company. The consultant can also promise and deliver anonymity to those expressing concerns.

Direction and Organization

A consultant has the important role of keeping the merger committee on the right track by reminding them about matters that need to be urgently solved. The consultant also drafts the time-line for the merger committee and reviews the time-line periodically to make sure that everything is progressing according to plan. Consultants have the experience in facilitating mergers and acquisitions, meaning that they will usually offer valuable advice to the merger committee.

Technology

There are several technological challenges to a merger or acquisition that a consultant can help in solving. Remember: the size of the firm will grow dramatically after the merger and there will likely be new challenges in areas such as telecommunications, data processing, telephone systems, accounting software and office equipment. All of these devices will need to be incorporated into the new company. A consultant can work with the administrative staff to design systems to support the new equipment without garnering any suspicion or mistrust.

Compensation of Partners

The two corporations involved in the acquisition or merger may have very different compensation systems. In this case, a consultant can help develop a new and custom-made system to replace the two different systems. The new system developed by the consultant should include all of the major provisions of the two former systems. Sometimes it makes sense to use different consultants for different portions of the pre-merger process. For example, an accounting firm may help with the preparation of the pro forma budget, while a public relations company helps with the marketing process. Any errors, omissions and other issues must be sorted out before signing contract documents. Consultants should always pay close attention to the legal matters.

XVIII. CONSULTING AGREEMENTS

Consultants are advised to read the terms and conditions of the consulting agreements carefully so that they do not feel short-changed should things go wrong. It has been noted that many consultant experts do not read the consulting contact agreements.

XIX. EMPLOYEE NUMBERS

According to WARN, any person who is working for the seller as of the effective date of the asset sale shall be taken as an employee of the purchasing company. When a large number of employees are to be terminated, the parties must consider the best time and place to do this. Consider what notice will be given and if there are any exceptions to be made, so as to avoid limited liability. Keep your state's WARN laws in mind during this process.

XX. ABSENTEEISM/SICKNESS RECORDS

YMSC (2009): During the sale process, you will be required to take into account any employees that are on sick leave. When the employee is not permanently disabled, give a return-to-work schedule to the employee, if possible. Ensure that new employees have life insurance coverage. Some companies have a life plan that requires the employees to be actively working before being covered. If your company plan cannot cover the new employees, encourage the affected employees to apply for a premium waiver. You can request that your life carrier address this issue through continuity of coverage.

Make sure to evaluate the company's disability plan. Most long-term disability contracts have limitations. Find out from your carrier whether they will waive pre-existing condition clauses or if they will apply credit for all the employees hired through the acquisition or merger. Where they are major differences in the benefit plans, the purchasing organization should take time to explain them well to employees.

Take time to evaluate the life insurance plan. Find out how you can factor in the employees who are absent from work during the time of sale due to sickness. It is a common practice to request the new carrier waive coverage for those employees who are at work to accommodate the new employees and hence make it possible for continuous life coverage.

XXI. EMPLOYEE MANUAL(S)

It is the duty of the new employer to make sure that all new employees get all the necessary information required by law. This information is usually provided during the new employee orientation process. In some organizations, such information is provided after the employee enrolls in the health plan. Even if you have a large number of new employees, this step should never be overlooked. The merger or acquisition is an ideal opportunity for you to offer sufficient information about procedures at the new company. This is best handled by promptly distributing an employee handbook or manual to all of the newly hired employees.

CONCLUSION

This manual has provided you with the tools required to carry out a successful negotiation for a merger or acquisition. A successful merger transaction starts with the creation of a merger committee that has the capacity to handle the details involved in the merger process. Investors are well advised never to handle the process on their own because it may lead to a disaster. The committee is more suitable because it can be made up of professionals with previous experience in handling such complex transactions.

The merger committee is responsible for acquiring new documents that prove the transfer of ownership. Some of these documents include: the articles of incorporation and the articles of association. There are other things that need to be ironed out such as bylaws to be followed by the two companies and proper shareholder communications. Generally, the steps listed in this manual will be sufficient to guide investors through the merger process.

REFERENCES

Accounting Tools (2012). Accounts Receivable Analysis. {Online}

Available: http://www.accountingtools.com/accounts-receivable-analysis

{Accessed}: 27th January, 2013.

Allen, L., Jagtiani, J., Perisiani, S. and Saunders, A. 2012. The Role of Advisors in Mergers and Acquisitions. New York: Baruch College Press.

Available: http://blog.investorrelations.com/2009/12/01/board-shareholder-communications/

{Accessed}: 22nd Jan 2013: 3:30pm

Anderson, M. (2002). *Mergers: A Practical Handbook. Part II. Anguilla: Edge International.* {Online}

Available: http://www.edge.ai/Edge-International-1057717.html

{Accessed}: 27th January, 2013.

Anderson, J. 1999. *People Management: The Crucial Aspect of Mergers.* {Online}

Available: http://irc.queensu.ca/gallery/1/cis-people-management.pdf

{Accessed}: 30th January, 2013.

AON, 2012. *Human Capital Consulting Mergers and Acquisitions Solutions.* {Online}

Available: http://www.aon.com/human-capital-consulting/consulting/mergers_acquisitions_solutions.jsp

{Accessed}: 30th January, 2013

Appelbaum, S., Gandell, J., Yortis, H., Proper, S. and Jobin, J. (2012). *Anatomy of a Merger: Behavior of Organizational factors and processes throughout the pre-during-post stages* (Part 1).

Bijilsma-Frankema, K. 2002. On Managing cultural Integration and cultural change processes in mergers and acquisitions. *Journal of European Industrial Training, Vol.25, April, pp. 192-207.*

Buono, A., Bowditch, J. 1989. *The Human Side of Mergers and Acquisitions.* San Francisco: Jossey-Bass. Board Source, 2007. *Executive Sessions: How to Use Them Regularly and Wisely.* Washington DC. {Online}

Available: (www.boardsource.org).

{Accessed}: 1st February, 2012.

Bilson, J. (2010). Accounts Payable Analysis for Entrepreneurs. {Online}.

http://suite101.com/article/accounts-payable-analysis-for-entrepreneurs-a201656

{Accessed}: 25th January, 2013.

Block, K., Dublin, B., and Wong, J. (2012). *Mergers and Acquisitions, Portfolio Purchasers and Vendor Programs*. Matthew Bender & Company Inc. {Online}.

Available: https://litigationessentials.lexisnexis.com/webcd/app?action=DocumentDisplay&crawlid=1&ptid=20079&lni=55H4-C6B0-0105-X064-00000-00&key=ea6be9c5b8073b6b5cdc7c5139ebf69e

California Secretary of State (2013). {Online}

Available: http://www.ftc.gov/speeches/other/dvpe-rumerg.shtm

Cartwright, S. and Cooper. C. 1992. *Mergers and Acquisitions the Human Factors*. Oxford: Butterworth-Heineman.

Cornell University, 2007. *A Legal Guide to Acquisitions and Doing Business in the United States*. New York: Baker & McKenzie

Creighton, S. and Sher, S. 2009.Resolving Patent Disputes through Merger: A Comparison of three potential Approaches. *Anti-Trust Law Journal*. {Online}

Available: http://www.wsgr.com/PDFSearch/creighton-sher0409.pdf

{Accessed}: 1st February, 2012.

Day, J.2008. *THEME: BAD DEBTS*. {Online}

Available: http://www.reallifeaccounting.com/pubs/Article_Theme_Bad_Debts.pdf

{Accessed}: 3rd February, 2013.

GA0. 2012. Government Audit. {Online}

Georgia Secretary of State (2012). *Non-compete law*. {Online}

Available: http://sos.georgia.gov/firststop/points_contact.pdf

{Accessed}: 4th February, 2012.

Hedley, A. 2013. *Getting Profit-Sharing Arrangements Right in a Merger*. {Online}

Available: http://www.managingpartner.com/node/6427

{Accessed}: 4th February, 2012.

Hirschfeld, S. 2010. *Labor and Employment Issues Triggered by Mergers and Acquisitions in the U.S.*

Federal Trade Commission (FTC).

Department of Justice (DOJ), (2012).

Independent Focus (2012).*Monthly Management Accounts.* {Online}

Available: https://www.findanaccountant.co.za/content_monthly-management-accounts

{Accessed}: 29th January, 2013.

Entrepreneur, 2013. *Your Business Plan Guide*. {Online}

http://www.entrepreneur.com/businessplan/index.html

Investopedia (2013). *Financial Statements: Revenue Recognition*. {Online}

Available: http://www.investopedia.com/exam-guide/
cfa-level-1/financial-statements/revenue-recognition.asp -
axzz2JgQjFbCx

Jeziorski, P. 2011. *Estimation of Cost Synersies from Mergers
Without cost data: Application to U.S. radio.* {Online}

Available: http://faculty.chicagobooth.edu/workshops/
marketing/PDF/costSynergiesPaper.pdf

{Accessed} 3rd February, 2013.

King & Spalding, 2012. *Insurance Checklist for Mergers and
Acquisitions: What Every Executive should Know.* {Online}

Available: http://www.kslaw.com/imageserver/KSPub-
lic/library/publication/ca120412.pdf

{Accessed} 3rd February, 2013.

Los Angles.2005. *Evaluation of Vendors/Contractors Engaged
in Mergers or Acquisitions.* {Online}

Available: http://countypolicy.co.la.ca.us/BOSPolicy-
Frame.htm

{Accessed} 3rd February, 2013.

Rylander, T. (2013). *Marketing Collateral.* {Online}

http://www.chooseamc.com/services/marketing-collater-
al/

Kang, D. and Mullineaux, D. 2011. *The Impact of Non-Bank
Lending on Mergers and Acquisitions.* {Online}

Available: http://papers.ssrn.com/sol3/papers.
cfm?abstract_id=1967126

{Accessed}: 3th February, 2013.

Kansas State University (2013). *Creating a Business Plan/ Financial Projections.* {Online}

Available:http://www.agmrc.org/business_development/ starting_a_business/creating_a_business/articles/mak-ing_financial_projections.cfm

Keythman, B. 2012. *How Should Extraordinary Gains & Losses Be Reported on the Income Statement?* {Online}

Available:**http://smallbusiness.chron.com/should-extraor-dinary-gains-losses-reported-income-statement-52040. html**

{Accessed}: 20th January, 2013. 2:00pm.

Kinsella, S. 2010. Intellectual Property and the Structure of Human Action. {Online}

Available: http://archive.mises.org/11383/intellectual-property-and-the-structure-of-human-action/

{Accessed}: 3th February, 2013.

Klees, E. and Horvitz, R. (2012). Consulting Agreements: The Good, the Bad, and the Ugly. *Journal Science.* {Online}

Available::http://sciencecareers.sciencemag.org/career_ magazine/previous_issues/articles/2012_10_12/caredit. a1200114

{Accessed}: 24th January, 2013.

Kuenyehia, K. (2010). *Seven Strategies of negotiation for M&A.* {Online}

Krishnan, C., Masulis, R., Thomas, R. and Thompson, R. 2011. *Litigation in Mergers and Acquitions.* {Online}

Available: http://sites.udel.edu/wccg/files/2011/10/SSRN-Thompson.pdf

{Accessed}: 24th January, 2013.

Marx, M., Singh, J.,and Fleming, L. 2012. *Regional Disadvantage? Non-Compete Agreements and Brain Drain.* {Online}

Available: http://www.iga.ucdavis.edu/Research/All-UC/conferences/berkeley-2012/fleming-paper-1

{Accessed}: 4th February, 2013.

Money-Zine (2012). *Understanding Stock Ownership.* {Online}

Available: http://www.money-zine.com/Investing/Investing/Understanding-Stock-Ownership/

{Accessed}: 24th January, 2013.

Myers, R. 2010. Know Your Sales Margin. {Online}

Available: http://www.entrepreneur.com/article/206390

{Accessed}: 4th February, 2013.

Shelly, E., Fields, L. and Webb (1997). An Investigation of Preferred Stock Financing by Bank and Non-bank financial Institutions. *Journal of Financial Research.*

Texas Secretary of State (2013). *Form 415: Amendments for Registration to Disclose change resulting from a conversion or merger.* {Online}

Available: http://www.sos.state.tx.us/corp/forms_boc.
shtml

{Accessed}: 4th January, 2013

Pushparaj, A. (2012). *What are Shares? Discuss the Types of Shares which a company can Issues.* {Online}

Available:http://www.publishyourarticles.net/knowl-
edge-hub/business-studies/what-is-shares-discuss-the-
types-of-shares-which-a-company-can-issue.html

{Accessed}: 24th January, 2013.

PwC (2012). *Revenue Recognition.* {Online}

Available: http://www.pwc.com/us/en/audit-assurance-
services/accounting-advisory/revenue-recognition.jhtml

{Accessed}: 24th January, 2013.

Russo, D. 2011. Mergers, Acquisitions, and Consolidations:
Managing Employment Tax Liability. *Journal of State Taxa-
tion.* {Online}

Available: http://www.talx.com/News/articles/Russo_
JSTA_29_06_11.pdf

{Accessed}: 4th January, 2013

Smith, S. (2013). *What is Stock Register?* WiseGeek. {Online}.

Available: http://www.wisegeek.com/what-is-a-stock-
register.htm

{Accessed}: 24th January, 2013.

Snow, B. 2012. *Keys to Successfully Completing an M&A Deal.* {Online}

Available: http://www.dummies.com/how-to/content/keys-to-successfully-completing-an-ma-deal.navId-811331.html

{Accessed}: 28th January, 2013.

State Corporation Commission, (2012). *Copies and Certificates.* {Online}

Available: http://www.scc.virginia.gov/clk/copy.aspx

{Accessed}: 28th January, 2013.

State of California. 2012. Business Filing. {Online}

Available: http://www.sos.ca.gov/business/be/filing-tips-corp.htm

{Accessed}: 20th January, 2013. 2:00pm.

State of Delaware(2013). *General Corporation Law.* {Online}

Available: http://delcode.delaware.gov/title8/c001/sc09/index.shtml

{Accessed}: 29th Jan, 2013. 20:50.

Tufts University .2013. Budget & Accounting. {Online}

http://finance.tufts.edu/budgetacc/budget-projections/

United States Department of Labor. 2012. Profit Sharing Plans for Small Businesses. {Online}

Available: http://www.dol.gov/ebsa/publications/profit-sharing.html

{Accessed}: 4th February, 2013.

TurboTax, 2012. *How Do I Request Prior Year Federal Tax Returns?* {Online}

Available: http://turbotax.intuit.com/tax-tools/tax-tips/IRS-Tax-Return/How-do-I-Request-Prior-Year-Federal-Tax-Returns-/INF14843.html

{Accessed}: 4th February, 2013.

Wilson, T. 2012. M&A: *How to Negotiate the Purchase or Sale of a Business.* {Online}

Available: http://www.avvo.com/legal-guides/ugc/ma-how-to-negotiate-the-purchase-or-sale-of-a-business

{Accessed} : 29th January, 2013.

Willsey, M. (2013). *How to Calculate your Draw on Sales Commissions.* {Online}

Investopedia, 2013. *Outstanding Warranties, options and securities.* {Online}

Available: http://www.investopedia.com/ask/answers/08/stock-option-warrant.asp - axzz2JgQjFbCx

Source: http://www.allbusiness.com/accounting-reporting/budget-budget-forecasting/2547-1.html - ixzz2JgmM6uBo

Wood, F. and Sangster, A. 2006. *Business Accounting 1.* Harlow: Pearson Education Limited.

Potential liability Potential liability Potential liability Potential liability Potential liability Potential liability

Wolff, M. 2013. *Board shareholder communications.* {Online}

YMSC, 2009. *Managing Mergers and Acquisitions.* Weston Parkway: Imma Institute. {Online}

Wilson, A., Braughler, L., and Tinga, R. 2009. *How to Deal with an Outstanding Warrant.* {Online}

Available: http://www.wikihow.com/Deal-With-an-Outstanding-Warrant

{Accessed}: 29th January, 2013.

Privacy Solutions. 2012. *VAT Registration for European Union Companies.* {Online}

Available:**http://www.privacy-solutions.com/vat-european-union.html**

{Accessed} : 4th February, 2013.

Spaulding, W. (2011). Option-like Securities — Callable Bonds, Convertible Securities, and Warrants.

Available: http://thismatter.com/money/options/option-like-securities.htm

{Accessed}: 29th January, 2013.

www.ingramcontent.com/pod-product-compliance
Lightning Source LLC
Chambersburg PA
CBHW060853280326
41934CB00007B/1036